# THE DECADENT WORLD-VIEW

## Borgo Press Books by BRIAN STABLEFORD

*Against the New Gods, and Other Essays on Writers of Imaginative Fiction*
*Algebraic Fantasies and Realistic Romances: More Masters of Science Fiction*
*Alien Abduction: The Wiltshire Revelations*
*The Best of Both Worlds and Other Ambiguous Tales*
*Beyond the Colors of Darkness and Other Exotica*
*Changelings and Other Metamorphic Tales*
*A Clash of Symbols: The Triumph of James Blish*
*Complications and Other Stories*
*The Cosmic Perspective and Other Black Comedies*
*Creators of Science Fiction*
*The Cure for Love and Other Tales of the Biotech Revolution*
*The Decadent World-View: Selected Essays*
*The Devil's Party: A Brief History of Satanic Abuse*
*The Dragon Man: A Novel of the Future*
*The Eleventh Hour*
*Exotic Encounters: Selected Reviews*
*Firefly: A Novel of the Far Future*
*Les Fleurs du Mal: A Tale of the Biotech Revolution*
*The Gardens of Tantalus and Other Delusions*
*Glorious Perversity: The Decline and Fall of Literary Decadence*
*Gothic Grotesques: Essays on Fantastic Literature*
*The Great Chain of Being and Other Tales of the Biotech Revolution*
*The Haunted Bookshop and Other Apparitions*
*Heterocosms: Science Fiction in Context and Practice*
*In the Flesh and Other Tales of the Biotech Revolution*
*The Innsmouth Heritage and Other Sequels*
*Jaunting on the Scoriac Tempests and Other Essays on Fantastic Literature*
*Kiss the Goat*
*Luscinia: A Romance of Nightingales and Roses*
*The Moment of Truth: A Novel of the Future*
*Narrative Strategies in Science Fiction, and Other Essays on Imaginative Fiction*
*News of the Black Feast and Other Random Reviews*
*An Oasis of Horror: Decadent Tales and Contes Cruels*
*Opening Minds: Essays on Fantastic Literature*
*Outside the Human Aquarium: Masters of Science Fiction, Second Edition*
*The Plurality of Worlds: A Sixteenth-Century Space Opera*
*Prelude to Eternity: A Romance of the First Time Machine*
*The Return of the Djinn and Other Black Melodramas*
*Salome and Other Decadent Fantasies*
*Slaves of the Death Spiders and Other Essays on Fantastic Literature*
*The Sociology of Science Fiction*
*Space, Time, and Infinity: Essays on Fantastic Literature*
*The Tree of Life and Other Tales of the Biotech Revolution*
*The Undead: A Tale of the Biotech Revolution*
*The World Beyond: A Sequel to S. Fowler Wright's The World Below*
*Yesterday's Bestsellers: A Voyage Through Literary History*

# THE DECADENT WORLD-VIEW

## Selected Essays

by

Brian Stableford

### The Borgo Press

*An Imprint of Wildside Press LLC*

**MMX**

*I.O. Evans Studies in the Philosophy and Criticism of Literature*
ISSN 0271-9061

**Number Fifty-Five**

Copyright © 1995, 1997, 1999, 2003, 2004, 2005, 2006, 2007, 2008, 2010 by Brian Stableford

All rights reserved.
No part of this book may be reproduced in any form without the expressed written consent of the publisher.

www.wildsidebooks.com

FIRST EDITION

# CONTENTS

Introduction ................................................................................. 7

THE DECADENT WORLD-VIEW
1. The Alchemical Marriage of Quasimodo and Esmeralda ......... 11
2. Miasmas and Perfumes .............................................................. 22
3. Beyond Paradise ......................................................................... 31
4. The Queen of Denial .................................................................. 42
5. Dandyism and the Splendor and Misery of Courtesans ............ 53
6. The Osmazome of Literature ..................................................... 63
7. The Devil's Departure ................................................................ 73
8. Twin Souls in Torment ............................................................... 85
9. Beyond Naturalism ..................................................................... 97
10. The Fruit of the Poisoned Tree ................................................ 107
11. Masked Lives ........................................................................... 117
12. The Next Best Thing ................................................................ 128
13. The Progress of Literary Satanism .......................................... 140
14. Decadence and the Novel of the Future ................................. 151

ADDENDA
15. Edgar Poe and the Gothic Lifestyle ........................................ 163
16. Fashions in Faithfulness: The Decadence of Ernest
    Dowson .................................................................................... 172
17. Should France's Angels have Revolted After All? ................ 180

Index ............................................................................................. 193
About the Author ......................................................................... 207

# INTRODUCTION

The fourteen articles featured here under the collective title of "The Decadent World-View" were originally published under that title, mostly in a slightly different form, as a regular feature in the magazine *Wormwood*, published twice a year by Tartarus Press. The original order was haphazard, and I have rearranged the items here so as to render it more nearly chronological. The whole series was, In effect, a series of extended footnotes to my previous study of decadence in literature, *Glorious Perversity: The Decline and Fall of Literary Decadence* (Borgo Press 1998). I have appended three other articles that might qualify as similar footnotes, although two were written before the book in question was published.

The purpose of the series was to explore in more detail a number of individual texts that were, of necessity, given only brief treatment in *Glorious Perversity*. Many of them take their cues from the list of recommended reading offered by Jean Des Esseintes in Joris-Kal Huysmans' *À rebours* (1884), which offered itself as a tongue-in-cheek handbook to the ideal decadent lifestyle. Such a recommendation is adequate evidence in itself that the books in question have a contribution to make to the world-view incarnated in such a lifestyle—a lifestyle that naturally includes far more reading than any more strenuous or exacting activity. The handful of texts that I have added to Des Esseintes' list were mostly produced by writers he complimented in general terms, although a few were published after *À rebours* and could not, in consequence, have featured therein. Although the series, seen as a whole, is inevitably patchy, I hope that it adds up to an appropriately fractured representation of the many-faceted world-view associated with those writers considered—with or without their own consent—to be the principal practitioners of "decadent style".

Although the general attributes of decadent style and the development of literary movement to which that idea gave birth are adequately introduced and summarized in the articles themselves, it might be appropriate to note here the fundamental principles of the decadent outlook. Just as literary Romanticism, of which literary Decadence was an offshoot, was framed as a revolt against literary Classicism, the exponents of decadent style always represented themselves as revolutionaries, developing new kinds of artifice in opposition to largely tacit conventional notions about how and why literary representation ought to be carried out. As Oscar Wilde pointed out, life imitates art far more than art imitates life, and that celebration of literary artifice was inevitably carried over into the lifestyle affectations of those writers who embraced the Decadent label most fervently—especially Charles Baudelaire, who became in consequence the flag-bearer and figurehead of the movement.

There is, of course, a certain ludicrousness in that kind of imaginative transference, but the exponents of decadent style in literature and lifestyle were defiantly unafraid of being accused either of madness, madness being so closely akin to genius in their eyes as to be a virtual qualification, or of perversity, perversity inevitably becoming a virtue in the light of calculatedly perverse judgment. In brief, the Decadent world-view revels in opposition and condemnation, taking almost all intended insults as compliments; the only accusation it cannot tolerate is an accusation of banal normality—but that is not an accusation to which its literary products ever lend themselves. That is why the subject-matter of this book is so interesting and intriguing, at least to me.

The articles in the main sequence originally appeared in the following issues of *Wormwood*: "The Alchemical Marriage of Quasimodo and Esmeralda" in number 11 (Autumn 2008); "Miasmas and Perfumes" in number 1 (2003); "Beyond Paradise" in number 7 (Autumn 2006) "The Queen of Denial" in number 4 (Spring 2005); "Dandyism and the Splendor and Misery of Courtesans" in number 9 (Autumn 2007) "The Osmazome of Literature" in number 3 (Autumn 2004) "The Devil's Departure" in number 2 (Spring 2004); "Twin Souls in Torment" in number 5 (Autumn 2005); "Beyond Naturalism" in number 8 (Spring 2007); "The Next Best Thing" in number 14 (Spring 2010); "The Fruit of the Poisoned Tree" in number 12 (Spring 2009); "Masked Lives" in number 6 (Spring 2006); "The Progress of Literary Satanism" in number 13 (Autumn 2009); and "Decadence and the Novel of the Future" in number 10 (Spring 2008). "Edgar Poe and the Gothic Lifestyle" first appeared in *Naked Truth* 4 (September 1995). "Fashions in Faithfulness" was written in April 1999, but I cannot recall who asked me to produce it, and I have no record of its ever being published. "Should France's Angels Have Revolted After All" first appeared in *The Penny Dreadfull* 9 (November 1997).

# I.

# THE ALCHEMICAL MARRIAGE OF QUASIMODO AND ESMERALDA

According to Arthur Koestler's analysis of *The Act of Creation*, the fundamental process of creativity is not a matter of creation *ex nihilo* but a particular kind of ordering process: the combination of ideas or images that were formerly disparate, but not necessarily chaotic, to form a new coherent whole. Whether this notion can really be universalized in the manner suggested by Koestler remains dubious, but the origin of the idea of literary decadence, as recognized and celebrated by this series of articles, certainly owes its origin to such a process of alchemical combination. When Théophile Gautier defined "the decadent style" in his introduction to the third edition of Charles Baudelaire's *Les Fleurs du Mal*, issued in 1868, he was cleverly fusing two ideas that had had not previously been bound together with such constructive elegance, although they could not be considered entirely unacquainted.

As Gautier was very well aware, the notion of "decadent style" had been introduced into French literary parlance more than thirty years before—initially in 1834, although it became much more prominent on its repetition two years later—by the critic Desiré Nisard, who intended it as a crushing insult. Nisard had appointed himself as a champion of Classicism against what he saw as the creeping menace of Romanticism, and had taken up arms in a bellicose fashion against Victor Hugo, the writer who had become the chief figurehead of the Romantic Movement in the 1830s, having taken over that role from the ailing Charles Nodier. Although it was not his first attack on Hugo to use the term, it was Nisard's article "M. Victor Hugo en 1836", which featured a determined assault on *Les Chants de crepuscule* [Twilight Songs] (1835), that provided the first detailed definition of "decadent style".

According to Nisard, the key symptoms of the literary rot that was supposedly setting in as the discipline, elegance and order of Classicism were tragically undermined, were a liking for profuse description, a preoccupation with detail, and—most important of all—an elevation of imaginative power over the stern restrictions of reason. All these things were, according to Nisard, direly unhealthy. He admitted that they were also rather seductive, especially the elaborate employment of the imagination, but that too he considered to be a bad thing.

Nisard did not accuse Hugo—not openly, at least—of any kind of moral decadence, but he and the greater part of his audience knew full well that *Les Chants du crepuscule*, like its immediate predecessor, *Les Feuilles d'automne* [Autumn Leaves] (1831), were attempts by Hugo to work through the tangled feelings consequent upon his marital difficulties, partly occasioned by his wife's liaison with Charles-Augustin Sainte-Beuve and partly by his own liaison with the actress Juliette Drouet. The same nexus of relationships produced another classic of proto-Decadent literature in Saint-Beuve's novel *Volupté*, published in 1834—the subject of the next article in the series.

There were, of course, many writers, critics and readers who thought that the aspects of Hugo's work criticized by Nisard were thoroughly good things. Initially, of course, their reaction was to deny the label along with the value-judgment and to refuse to accept that such stylistic adventures were in any way "decadent". Others, however—most prominent among them Charles Baudelaire—took a different tack, turning the intended insult into a wry compliment by using the word "decadent" as if it were an item of praise. Baudelaire, with typical perversity, was perfectly happy to use the term in his own critical writings as a compliment, not only to describe the work of Victor Hugo but also that of Richard Wagner—and he was more than content for his own work to be considered and described as "decadent".

Equally typically, Baudelaire took up Nisard's definition of decadent style and extrapolated it, introducing further elaborations and complications to the description. In Baudelaire's view, the key to the merit and timeliness of decadent style was the willingness of literary and other artists to accept and develop influences from other artistic fields than their own, forming new kinds of connections and partnerships between literature, music and the visual arts. His interest in prose poetry was one example of this enthusiasm for creative hybridization, and his interest in "dandyism" as a means of importing exotic artistry into a lifestyle was another—and both were interests that anticipated Koestler's theory of creativity in intriguing ways.

Given Baudelaire's usurpation of Nisard's terminology and Gautier's exceedingly strong interest in exactly those stylistic features of Romanticism of which Nisard disapproved so sternly, it is hardly surprising that Gautier took up the notion of decadent style in his introduction to the posthumous omnibus edition of *Les Fleurs du Mal*. Nor is it suprising that he too attempted to take the notion further, not only by making newly grandiose claims for it, but by producing an even more elaborate and carefully recomplicated definition of its features. He was, however assisted in that work by the recent popularization of another set of ideas, similarly produced in conscious opposition to Nisard's, but coming from a very different direction. It was Gautier's fusion of the existent notion of decadent style with this new set of ideas that completed the theory of literary Decadence and made it so potent as a source of future influence and the seed of an explicit movement.

Nisard summarized his ideas regarding the evolution of literature in a multi-volume *Histoire de la littérature française*, issued between 1844 and 1861, the concluding volume of which delivered his final verdict on Victor Hugo and the other pillars of the French Romantic Movement. The entire work was, of course, a ringing defense of Classicism as the acme of progressive literary artistry, as developed by literary geniuses standing on the shoulders of giant predecessors, and its conclusion bitterly regretted the apparent decay of the ideals and achievements of Classicism in the resistible, but lamentably uninhibited, rise of Romanticism. It was, in many ways, a kind of literary history that is still typical today, which regards literature as a more-or-less closed domain, entire of itself and more than self-sufficient. It emerged, however, in an era in which new kinds of history were being imagined and written: scientific histories—or, in French terms, "positive" histories, in the great intellectual tradition of the grand theorist of positivism, August Comte. Such works conscientiously went in search of theories in which the evolution of literature could only be one aspect of a much more general evolutionary process, in which cause-and-effect replaced the sequential innovations and interventions of genius.

Three years after the appearance of the concluding volume of Nisard's monumental history, Hippolyte Taine published his *Histoire de la littérature anglaise*, which adopted the Comtean approach with an unprecedentedly brazen verve, claiming that the history of English literature—and, by extrapolation, the history of all literature—was explicable in scientific terms, as a product of three causal factors, which Taine termed "*race, milieu et moment*". These terms have never been easy to translate, and the confusion as to their precise frames of reference is only confused by the fact that all three words also exist in English, with markedly different frames of reference to the ones they embrace in French common parlance, let alone the specific operational definitions devised for the sake of Taine's thesis.

Taine's "race" does not mean race in a broad sense, or even (as it is sometimes translated) "nation", but is actually much more closely connected with the etymological origin of the term, which means "root"; the best available translation of the term might be "heredity". It refers to the fact that a writer has a particular inheritance of influence by virtue of his family's history—not merely its present social position but its members' awareness of past changes in that social situation.

"Milieu" translates accurately enough into "environment", but it includes both physical and social aspects of the environment as well as a writer's idiosyncratic life-experiences, and is inevitably respectful of a writer's particular literary environment, in terms of what is prestigious, popular and publishable.

"Moment" is sometimes translated as "epoch" but that does not really help; the term does not simply mean the particular historical date at which a writer produces a work, or even the location of that date within a discernible "period" of history, but implies a context in which both the date and the period are envisaged as being parts and examples of an unfolding historical process. For Taine, "moments" are not merely points or ranges on the axis of a graph but elements of an unfolding story, each one not merely intelligibly related to earlier and later points and ranges, but actively bridging them. Thus, the crucial implication of this notion is that every historical era, whether broadly or narrowly defined, is pregnant with its own potential contributions not only to the artistic recognition of change but the artistic furtherance of that change.

In terms of Taine's theory, as in many others, literature is alive and active as a historical force rather than merely providing a mirror for the purposes of self-criticism or self-admiration, but its action and power are not so much products of individual artistic genius as they are of more basic and more generalized forces and impulses. By the time he published his literary history, Taine was already famous for the oft-quoted dictum that "*le vice et la vertu sont des produits comme le vitriol et le sucre*" [vice and virtue are products, like sulfuric acid and sugar], and he imagined literature as one of the "factories" involved in that production as a matter of routine.

It was the recent popularization of Taine's point of view that encouraged Gautier to combine the notion of "decadence" popularized by Desiré Nisard with another notion of "decadence" popularized in France by the Baron de Montesquieu, author of *Considérations sur les causes de la grandeur des Romains et de leur décadence* (1774). Montesquieu had already drawn parallels between ancient Rome and modern France, which had come to seem uncomfortably prophetic in the century following their publication, as the grandeur of France's *ancien régime* had given way to corruption, revolution, hopeful revival, further revolution and farcical revival, on the way—although Gautier could only anticipate that in 1868, two years before the battle of Sedan and the Paris Commune—to its final ignominious collapse. Montesquieu had not suggested that all decadent empires would produce literature with certain key stylistic similarities, but that was an inevitable corollary of Taine's thesis, and that corollary moved Gautier to assert that Baudelaire's decadent style (as well as, tacitly, his own and Victor Hugo's) was a natural and expectable product of its historical moment, albeit extrapolated by Baudelaire (as well as, tacitly, by himself and Victor Hugo) to a new, particularly fine and epoch-making extreme.

Although Gautier did not express his thesis in strict Tainean terminology, the very essence of his notion of Decadent style is that it is a product of particularly-rooted and particularly-situated artists at a particular historical moment: in brief, that Decadent style is the veritable product of a decadent historical era, as perceived and embodied by artists shaped by heredity and experience to be particularly and acutely sensitive to that historical decadence. There is not an atom of doubt that Baudelaire—who had always blamed his *ennui, spleen, impuissance* and literary genius on exactly such a nexus of cruel circumstances and quasi-heroic response—would have agreed with him wholeheartedly. Gautier's other hero, Victor Hugo, might have dissented in matters of detail—he never accepted the "decadent" label, always considering it mistaken as well as insulting—but he would surely have agreed with the broader terms of Gautier's argument, particularly with reference to its Tainean component. We can be reasonably certain of this because Hugo had anticipated many of the argument's elements in his own critical writings and exemplified them graphically in his works; indeed, one of the most remarkable anticipatory celebrations of the Tainean notion of "moment" can be found in Hugo's novel *Notre-Dame de Paris—1482*, first published in 1831, whose original title took the unusual step of including a specifying date (an inclusion routinely omitted from citations and later editions).

Hugo set out his own manifesto for Romanticism in the preface to the published version of the then-unperformed play *Cromwell* (1827). There, in addition to celebrating exactly the same artistic strategies that Nisard—who had read the preface in question—was later to decry, Hugo specifically identified crucial phases in human history with distinctive artistic forms, culminating in modern drama, and, more particularly, the new kind of Romantic drama with which he was explicitly attempting to revolutionize a theater steeped in Classicism. Although *Cromwell* did not succeed in precipitating that revolution, *Hernani* (1830) did—aided, in no uncertain terms, by the combative claque that turned out mob-handed to its first night performance, led by Théophile Gautier, clad in a calculatedly-scandalous red waistcoat. Hugo also took exception in the preface to *Cromwell* to the Classicist notion that the primary, and perhaps sole, function of art was to embody and develop the aesthetic principle of beauty; he argued, forcefully, that artists should no longer attempt to exclude frank ugliness from their work, or repress it by treating it as an implicit evil, and that they should instead make a concerted attempt to accommodate the alternative aesthetic principles of the sublime and the grotesque within their works. *Notre-Dame de Paris* attempts to develop this thesis in a characteristically flamboyant fashion.

One of the consequences of the temporary flourishing of a Romantic Movement in England was to encourage a subsequent distinction between long prose fictions described as "novels" and those described as "romances", the former adopting a new aesthetic goal of verisimilitude with regard to their descriptions of human social life while the latter continued, or renewed, an older storytelling tradition in which, to use Nisard's terminology, the power of the imagination was elevated above and beyond the stern restrictions of reason. That distinction was not made in France, where the word that ultimately came to mean "novel" was, in fact, *roman*, but there was an awareness nevertheless of an increasing distinction between "realistic" narratives and more fanciful ones. The ambiguity of the tern *roman* probably helped to emphasize this problematic contrast rather than overruling its significance. At any rate, Hugo—in sharp contrast to Charles Nodier—was intensely and specifically interested in hybridizing the "novelistic" and the "romantic" tendencies of the *roman*, in the hope of producing a new literary center-ground. *Notre-Dame de Paris* was the first of several attempts to do that, and although *Les Misérables* (1862) is generally reckoned to be his most successful masterpiece, there is an argument for considering its ground-breaking predecessor as the more remarkable achievement.

Traditionally, pre-nineteenth-century historical romances had been set in a generalized mythical past whose settings were largely arbitrary, and which routinely permitted supernatural intrusions. When they borrowed datable historical incidents for use as artistic motifs and plot-structures, they tended to transplant them into a generalized narrative space in which the differences between, for example, ancient Rome, Renaissance Europe and the Age of Enlightenment were minimized, if not erased. Hugo's essential purpose was, however, to modernize romance by transplanting it into a well-defined historical past, with a highly specific setting, from which the supernatural had been banished in actuality even though it still held enormous influence in common belief—and, by virtue of that fact, permitted characters to imagine themselves, and construe their experiences, in essentially supernatural terms.

The novel's full title is thrown into even sharper focus by a remarkable rhapsodic essay introduced into the story by the loquacious narrative voice—an intrusion of which Desiré Nisard must have strongly disapproved and disdained—which argues that the year 1482 lay on a significant historical cusp, by virtue of the fact that "the book of architecture" was about to be replaced by "the book of printing" as the chief mode of cultural communication. The invention of the printing-press by Gutenberg had actually taken place a generation before, but it was not until after Gutenberg's death that presses began to spread like wildfire throughout Europe. 1482 is an adequate definition of that revolutionary event, although the main reason for its specific selection as the novel's momentary setting is that it was final year of the reign of Louis XI; Louis figures in the novel as a character whose pernicious influence, symbolic of the last gasp of Medievalism, is on the brink of termination.

What the argument of this inserted essay asserts is that in a fundamentally preliterate era, in which reading and writing were the preserve of churchmen and a tiny supplementary élite of church-educated laymen, the chief communicator of the Medieval church's world-view to the broader population was its architecture. In 1482 the cathedral of Notre-Dame de Paris was, therefore, a kind of "showcase anthology" in which the layers of Medieval thought expressed in the city had been secreted in stone—an anthology whose strata were still preserved in the edifice in 1831, albeit having been overlaid by further exemplary layers. After 1482, however, the inexorable spread of printing-presses had gradually transferred the burden of the cathedral's responsibility to the printed book—which, by slow degrees, the entire population of France had learned to read. The date of the novel's appearance is, in the context of this argument, just as important as the date of the story's setting, bracketing that historical process.

Implicit within the argument, of course, is the suggestion that the ambition of *Notre-Dame de Paris—1482*, as a historical artifact, is to be nothing less than a modern Notre-Dame de Paris: a microcosm of Paris, and hence of civilization. Although its events are confined to a matter of long-elapsed months and a handful of rather bizarre characters, the manner in which those characters behave—or, more accurately, are seen to behave by the relentlessly modern eye whose imagined sense-data fuel the narrative voice—embodies the dynamic thrust of a rich pattern of historical and literary evolution.

The process of hybridization by which Hugo attempts to fuse past and present, history and romance, and visionary and literary imagery, is no mere matter of juxtaposition, but something more akin to the "alchemical marriage" symbolically described in the Rosicrucian pamphlet signed by Johann Valentin Andreae, *Chymische Hochzeit Christiani Rosenkreutz* [The Chemical Wedding of Christian Rose-Cross] (1616), which appealed for a new fusion of natural science and occult science, in the characteristically holistic spirit of the latter. Hugo subsequently became a wholehearted subscriber to that cause, in the spirit of the nineteenth-century occult revival, and *Notre-Dame de Paris* is notable not only for its fascinated descriptions of what would now be called "alternative states of consciousness" but also its use of such states as the significant levers of the novel's plot. The tragedy of that plot hinges, and eventually culminates, in a "wedding" that has to be supernatural because it cannot possibly be social: that of the story's hero and heroine, Quasimodo and Esmeralda. Although they cannot be united in life, their skeletons are found seductively entwined long after the innocent Esmeralda—notionally a gypsy girl but actually the mislaid daughter of a masochistic aspirant saint—has been brutally put to death for a murder that Quasimodo's protector, Claude Frollo, has committed in a hallucinatory rage of frustration.

The alternative title by which *Notre-Dame de Paris* is generally known in English, *The Hunchback of Notre Dame*, has a certain propriety by virtue of this key relationship between Quasimodo and Emeralda. Quasimodo the hunch-backed bell-ringer was by no means the first strategically-deformed character invented by Hugo in order to pursue the aim expressed the preface to *Cromwell* of leavening the beautiful with the hideous for aesthetic reasons—his early novellas, *Bug-Jargal* and *Han d'Islande* [Hans of Iceland], written in his teens but not published until after *Notre-Dame de Paris*, both contain similar characters—but he was the first to present such a strident defiance of the common aesthetic stratagem of equating ugliness with moral vice. Quasimodo is by no means a moral paragon, but he has a far purer moral intelligence than the scholarly Claude Frollo, the outrageously handsome Captain Phoebus, the corrupt King Louis XI, or even the scatterbrained Pierre Gringoire, each of whom has a less heroic or outrightly villainous role to play in Esmeralda's tragedy. Hugo was to take this particular device to even further lengths, and perhaps to a higher perfection, in the magnificently grotesque and wrathful *L'Homme qui rit* [The Man Who Laughs] (1869), but he hesitated twice over in formulating the latter novel, first by setting his story in England and secondly by giving the hideous hero a blind lover incapable of perceiving his stigmata. Quasimodo and Esmeralda do not have that contrived advantage, and their tortured relationship is all the stronger for its frank impossibility.

Quasimodo is explicitly established within the novel as a symbolic personification of the cathedral. Just as the actual Notre-Dame de Paris is a stratified patchwork, replete with Gothic flourishes and gargoyles that are part and parcel of its embodiment of the problematic evolution of Christian ideals, its bell-ringer too is a patchwork of robust athleticism and physical disability, whose experience and consciousness of affection and cruelty, and beauty and loathing, exemplify a similarly complex and confused—but nevertheless progressive—evolution. Nor is this analogy restricted to the edifice and the character; it also extends, at least to some extent, to the text itself. The "replacement cathedral" of the printed text is itself a calculatedly hectic accumulation, meandering in its direction and elaborated by all manner of strange narrative inclusions, not merely heavy on description, detail and imaginative power, but in reflective commentary on its own nature.

*Notre-Dame de Paris* is by no means an ugly or misshapen book, but it is a loud, assertive and intoxicated book, which robustly exalts the power of the imagination over the stern restrictions of reason. Like Quasimodo, it is utterly deaf to the everyday prattle of critical mortals like Desiré Nisard, but it can feel, if not hear, the music of the bells ringing out their summons to the great flock of humankind, inviting them to worship, in the twilight as well as the dawn. For that reason, it is a highly significant anticipation of the world-view that Baudelaire, Gautier and all their myriad followers were later to embrace as "Decadent"—because rather than in spite of the intended ugliness of the word.

## II.

## MIASMAS AND PERFUMES

In Théophile Gautier's definition, framed in his introduction to the posthumous third edition of Charles Baudelaire's *Les Fleurs du Mal*, literary decadence is "Art arrived at that point of extreme maturity that determines civilizations which have grown old; ingenious, complicated, clever, full of delicate hints and refinements, gathering all the delicacies of speech, borrowing from technical vocabularies, taking color from every palette, tones from all musical instruments, contours vague and fleeting, listening to translate subtle confidences, confessions of depraved passions and the odd hallucinations of a fixed idea turning to madness". Such a style is, according to Gautier, "summoned to express all and to venture to the very extremes". Baudelaire's work partakes of "language already veined with the greenness of decomposition"—but that is allegedly inevitable, in a civilization "where an artificial life has replaced a natural one and developed in a man who does not know his own needs."

Gautier was writing in advance of the development of naturalism, and would have been horrified to learn that novelistic depictions of everyday life were fated to replace lyric poetry as the principal medium of French literary artistry. From his viewpoint, Decadent style had to be seen in contrast to Classical style, and was far more liberal in terms of its contents because "it admits of backgrounds where the spectres of superstition, the haggard phantoms of dreams, the terrors of night, remorse which leaps out and falls back noiselessly, obscure fantasies that astonish the day, and all that the soul in its deepest depths and innermost caverns conceals of darkness, deformity and horror, move together confusedly." Paradoxically—and therefore very appropriately—the text that had more influence than any other on Baudelaire's own world-view and style was itself a novel that can nowadays be seen as a significant precursor of naturalism: *Volupté* (1834) by Charles-Augustin Sainte-Beuve.

Sainte-Beuve was aware of the fact that Baudelaire idolized him, but was by no means grateful for the honor; when Baudelaire asked his advice about offering himself as a candidate for the Académie Française in 1861, Sainte-Beuve told him, frostily, not to bother. Sainte-Beuve thought that Baudelaire had seriously misunderstood the moral of *Volupté*—an opinion based on an "epistle" written (in verse) in 1844, in which Baudelaire proclaimed that he had imported the story of Amaury into his heart, absorbing all its "miasmas" and "perfumes", and that he had become a practitioner of the same "cruel art" as its protagonist.

That, according to Sainte-Beuve, was *"folie"* (madness)—a judgment which he, as the great pioneer of psychoanalytical literary criticism, felt perfectly competent to make. Sainte-Beuve was, however, the critic who thought that Balzac, Stendhal and Flaubert were also a trifle deranged, as well as second-rate by comparison with such true giants of contemporary French literature as Pierre-Jean de Béranger (whom Baudelaire publicly despised) and Ernest Feydeau (the father of the now-more-famous *farceur*); it is surely possible that he was as mistaken in his estimation of his own work as he was of Baudelaire's.

The seed of *Volupté* was sown in the first and most influential of all the literary *salons* of Paris, which was hosted by Charles Nodier at the Bibliothéque de l'Arsenal following his appointment as librarian in 1824. Nodier's *salon* was the cradle of the French Romantic Movement and its *cénacles*, and the venue in which Nodier (who had been born in 1780) handed the banner of that movement over to his successor as its presiding genius, Victor Hugo (born in 1802). Gautier (born in 1811) was too young to be a participant, but Alfred de Vigny (born in 1797) and Alexandre Dumas (born in 1802) were regulars—and so was Charles Sainte-Beuve (born in 1804).

It was at Nodier's *salon* that Sainte-Beuve and Victor Hugo became close friends, and at the spinoff *cénacle* at Hugo's house in the rue Notre-Dame-des-Champs that the former met the latter's wife, Adèle, with whom he fell in love. According to rumour, Adèle became Sainte-Beuve's mistress in 1833, the early phases of their affair coinciding exactly with the writing of *Volupté*.

*Volupté* is not a *roman à clef*; Monsieur de Couaën, is certainly not a representation of Victor Hugo, and is probably as different from the poet as Sainte-Beuve could contrive. The Irish-born Madame de Couaën is not a recognisable representation of Adéle, and the biography of her admirer, Amaury, is not markedly similar to that of the author. Nor, so far as we can tell, is the description of Amaury's chaste "affair" with Madame de Couaën an accurate representation of Sainte-Beuve's actual dealings with Adèle Hugo. On the other hand, one may certainly suppose that the novel's description of Amaury's *feelings* is, in some fashion, as painstakingly accurate as its author could contrive; the whole purpose of the text, as its preface stridently declares, is "to analyze a tendency—call it a passion, even a vice—and the part of the soul that this vice dominates and colors: the part that is languishing, idle, clinging, secret and private, mysterious and furtive, dreamy to the point of over-refinement, tender to the point of laxity; in short, the sensual, voluptuous part."

The difference between Sainte-Beuve and Baudelaire is easy to understand in terms of the attitudes they adopted to the subject-matter of the book. Amaury tells his story from a point of view that is twenty years later than the conclusion of the events described and nearly thirty years after their beginning; by the time he makes his confession he is a bishop in the Catholic Church and he is writing it *en route* to America, his new fatherland. He intends his story to be a cautionary tale, stern advice against surrender to temptation—even though the vice to which Amaury actually surrenders is not the one that tempts him at all, but a more generalized "displacement activity" whose description is so vague that it is credited more to the city of Paris than any of its inhabitants. From Sainte-Beuve's viewpoint, the dominant emotion of the book is guilt; the whole thing is an attempt to explain not merely how Amaury was tempted, but how he overcame temptation, with some assistance from the cathartic effect of literature. Baudelaire saw things differently; for him, it was the young Amaury, not the old, who is the hero of the tale, and it is the temptation, not its ultimate vanquishment, that provides the heart and soul of the narrative.

There is, perhaps, a sense in which Baudelaire—who regarded himself as an "incorrigible Catholic" and loved the work of Edgar Allan Poe—might have done better to go into the Church and/or emigrate to America, but he simply could not do either. He could not tear himself away from Paris, and he was so firmly committed to the adversary delineated by his faith that he wrote a "Litany to Satan". For him, the young Amaury was a man who had seen through the sham of French bourgeois existence and realised the hopeless inadequacy of morality to contain or defeat the insistent promptings of the inner self.

It is hardly surprising that Baudelaire should have taken this view. Was this not, after all, what the Romantic Movement was supposed to be all about? The core of Romantic philosophy was its resistance to Classicism's premature celebration of the victory of reason and order over emotion and chaos; Romantic art insisted instead on the relative impotence of the conscious mind to dominate or ameliorate the unruly forces of the unconscious mind: the fountainhead of all the passions, whose most powerful jet is lust.

Because Sainte-Beuve knew this, *Volupté* is saturated with the assumptions and ideals of Romanticism—but because Sainte-Beuve was not wholehearted in his own Romanticism, the saturation is symptomatic of the deep anxiety that eventually led him to become a veritable bishop among literary critics. He became a meddlesome cleric who looked deep into the souls of men, through the only reliable lens there is—far more accurate in its estimations than the confessional—only to be horrified by what he found there. It required a Baudelaire to follow the chain of reasoning set out in *Volupté* to its logical end—which was, of course, to embrace everything of which the not-so-young Sainte-Beuve was terrified, and to accept the damnation to which the young Amaury would have been condemned, had he not repented his troublesome ways.

Sainte-Beuve's greatest mistake, from his own viewpoint—or his greatest good fortune, from Baudelaire's—was to have written

Amaury's story as a novel. Even in an epic poem, John Milton—without knowing it, according to William Blake—had demonstrated that as soon as one attempts to explain and understand the devil's motives, in the interests of depicting him more accurately, one risks the possibility that one's readers might sympathizing with those motives. When *Volupté* was written, novelistic narrative had not yet been refined by Flaubert and his successors to the point at which minimally-distant third-person narrative could maximize the identification between reader and protagonist, but Sainte-Beuve's first-person narrative never achieves the scrupulous distance to which it aspires. The simple fact is that the tale's real teller has far more in common with young Amaury than the alleged teller (old Amaury) has with either of them—with the result that the reader (you, me or Baudelaire) is in a far better position to understand and sympathize with young Amaury than with old Amaury.

To a sensitive reader, old Amaury is a mere inconvenience, who would get in the way if we let him, so we pay no attention to him; we pretend that he is not really there—as we are surely entitled to do, given that the real author is not only pretending to be absent from his own text but is doing so by perversely substituting a crabby old bore for his own potentially-more-interesting presence. Since the real author is in hiding, we can listen to his authentic voice—which is, of course, far more honest than any public *persona* he might adopt were we unlucky enough to meet him in person or hear him in the confessional.

We, as readers, can easily sort out the honest elements of *Volupté* from the dishonest ones, even though its author never could. We can see that, if only his creator were not such a stupid prig, Amaury might not feel forced to displace his passion from its true object (Madame de Couaën) to some vague guilt-stricken self-indulgence in the gutters of Paris—and we are therefore free to wonder what he might and should have done instead.

The vulgar answer, of course, would have been to persist in his attempted seduction of Madame de Couaën until her virtuous resistance broke down. That, at least according to rumor, is what Sainte-Beuve actually did in respect of Adèle Hugo—but we hardly need old Amaury to tell us that there is something irredeemably *de trop* about a young aspirant Romantic screwing *Victor Hugo's wife*. Because we are not merely civilized folk but folk aware of the irredeemable decadence of modern civilization, we (you, me and Baudelaire, that is) are bound to reach a different conclusion: one that even Charles Sainte-Beuve discovered, although not wholeheartedly enough. That conclusion is that the proper disposition of such passions is neither displacement activity nor sublimation, but literary activity.

We can see, although Sainte-Beuve could not and old Amaury therefore would not, that Amaury's narration of his story not only ought to be, but actually *is* his reward, rather than his pretended punishment. We, unlike Sainte-Beuve, have arrived at a maturity that, instead of being stuck in clerical mud, is ingenious, complicated, clever, full of delicate hints and refinements: one that can gather all the delicacies of speech and borrow from technical vocabularies, colourful palettes and musical tones in order to translate subtle confidences and confessions of depraved passions—and maybe even the odd hallucinations of fixed ideas turning to *folie*. At least, we could if we were Baudelaire—and if we aren't, we surely ought to try as hard as we can to pretend.

*Volupté* is, in consequence of providing scope to be read in this way, a pivotal text in the history of the French novel. It was the last echo of the Jean-Jacques Rousseau-inspired cult of *sensibilité* [sensitivity], which gave French Romanticism its distinctive tint; it was also the departure-point of a new literary tradition that culminated, in spite of its author's attempts to steer a safer course for nineteenth-century French literature, in the Decadent and Symbolist movements. Within its pages, Rousseauesque *sensibilité* evolves—or decays—into *sensuality*, the closest translation of the word *volupté* that English can provide. That not only renders its users sensitive to the uncontrollable elements of nature but gives them a new kind of transformative power over those elements: a power that requires to be contrasted with "control".

What so impressed Baudelaire about Amaury was not so much his capacity to feel—his passion and his vice—but his capacity to project that feeling outwards, to impose it upon the world by mentally transforming its landscapes and edifices, and the weather that disturbs them, into allegorical representations of the irrational element of the human psyche.

The first phase of Amaury's psychic odyssey takes him from La Gastine, an isolated farmhouse in a remote part of Brittany—a calculatedly unostentatious one-storey edifice set in a fertile plain, interrupted by beech-trees, which symbolizes the quiet desolation of conventional rural existence—to the Château de Couaën, a house set in more precipitous country near a barren coast. The château is just as remote as La Gastine, but even more ancient; it served in a long-gone era as a fortress, and its tower and ramparts survive, although it now plays host to futile secret gatherings of the anti-Revolutionary nobility. The Marquis' study, library and bedroom occupy an upper floor whose garret is a rat-infested granary, but Madame Couaën's room is full of polished antique furniture, porcelain and Irish crystal, where everything seems to be lustrous, if not luminous.

Madame Couaën's self-imposed duties include the maintenance of Saint-Pierre-de-Mer, a mountain chapel overlooking a boulder-strewn bay, which reminds her of her native Ireland. The ruins of a stone watch-tower stand on the edge of the cliff (which her husband decides to convert into a lighthouse after her death). It is at Saint-Pierre that Amaury's long obsession with the imagery of water begins; once he has been there he continually thinks of human emotions in terms of their analogy with bodies of water, afflicted by tides and waves. At one point he imagines the souls of the Couaëns as an allegorical painting whose centrepiece is a calm but misty lake, fed by streams overflowing into waterfalls, echoing Madame Couaën's contradictory response to Saint-Pierre. (It is significant that when Amaury first sets out for America, the tempestuous ocean drives his ship back to the Portuguese shore.)

Before Amaury sets off for Paris, modernity manifests itself within his native landscape as an intrusion, in the form of Monsieur Vacquerie's house, whose facilities include a Barbary organ, an opticon and a microscope. When he goes to the capital he and the Couaëns remain on the outskirts of the city, initially staying in a small religious community near Val-de-Grâce (whose famous convent became a military hospital), and later in Auteuil. Paris seems ostentatious and feverish to Amaury; the only aspect of his obsessive peregrinations that does not aggravate his sensuality is his excursions to the Jardin des Plantes to hear the Chevalier de Lamarck expound his theory of evolution—whose world-view seems to him unnecessarily stark and dolorous. He eventually finds solace, however, in a library of religious works. When he finally achieves calm of mind he envisages himself afloat on a placid sea, approaching a new shore, which is *not* the shore of Druid Island (an islet off the Breton coast, reputedly a sacred site of Druid religion but subsequently pockmarked by the ruins of a Christian monastery), where he had earlier imagined himself living in exile—a plan he quickly abandoned when he discovered how intimidating the island became after nightfall.

The modern reader has no difficulty at all in recognising the methods of literary symbolism at work within this plot, just as the modern reader is likely to side with Baudelaire in regretting old Amaury's preference for calm inshore waters over stormy open seas, and his retirement to a dusty religious library rather than Druid Island. Even in 1834, readers would have become familiar with the conventional symbolism of landscape and weather by reading Gothic novels—particularly, in France, the best-selling translations of works of Ann Radcliffe. In Gothic novels, however, the symbolism is contingent, alarmist and frankly melodramatic; it may reflect the emotional turmoil of the characters but it does not interact with that turmoil in the complex fashion of *Volupté*, and no Gothic heroine ever attempted to conduct a rigorous self-examination, let alone a constructive self-extrapolation, by managing that symbolism. Baudelaire cannot have been the only reader who was entranced by Amaury's method even while deploring his objective, nor the only one who realized—in spite of the author's intentions—that it was the method, not the objective, that was worthy of emulation.

The use of water as a defining symbolic element was by no means original to Sainte-Beuve. Although he disapproved of Balzac, he must have read *La Peau de chagrin* (1830) and he was a sufficiently sensitive reader to have taken note of the manner in which bodies of water and the flow of water assist in the construction of a commentary on its unfortunate hero's changing fortunes and state of mind. In Balzac too, however, the symbolism is contingent, an arbitrary artifice contrived by an impersonal narrative voice. Amaury's symbolism is more intimate and more active; water is *his* choice as a symbolic scheme; it is not merely the meaning of what he sees but actually *what he sees* that is transformed by his active involvement in symbolic construction and interpretation. When he imagines the Couaëns' souls as a painting, he is an artist; when he tells his story, he is not making any mere confession. Baudelaire could see that with perfect clarity; so, in his turn, could Stéphane Mallarmé, the great theorist of literary symbolism.

Baudelaire was entirely correct, therefore, when he claimed that he had imported the true story of Amaury into his heart by means of absorbing its miasmas and perfumes—ignoring its ostensible moral—and that the faculty of which he was about to become a definitive practitioner was the same "cruel art". Far from being *folie*, this was perfect sanity, albeit of a kind that was prepared, and determined, to venture to extremes—in a world where an artificial life had already replaced a natural one and alienated people from their own needs—and did not hesitate to admit of backgrounds where the spectres of superstition, the haggard phantoms of dreams, the terrors of night and all that the soul conceals of darkness, deformity and horror, moved together. Did they do so confusedly? Well, perhaps—but in art, confusion is not always what it seems, any more than an explicit moral has to coincide with a tacit one.

In sum, *Volupté* is a far better book than its author intended, provided that it reaches a reader capable of seeing the deluge instead of the raindrops.

# III.

## BEYOND PARADISE

Charles Baudelaire's longest prose work, *Les Paradis artificiels*, was published in 1860, three years after the first edition of *Les Fleurs du mal*. The book has two parts; the first, "La poème du haschisch," is an essay on the effects of that drug, while the second, "Un mangeur d'opium", is a commentary on Thomas De Quincey's two accounts of the effects of laudanum—a solution of opium extracts in alcohol, which became the nineteenth century's most popular pain-killer. The first of these accounts, *Confessions of an Opium Eater*, had been published in the *London Magazine* in 1821 and translated into French by Alfred de Musset in 1828, while parts of the second, the incomplete *Suspiria de Profundis*, had been published by *Blackwood's* in 1845. Baudelaire had published an earlier essay, "Du vin et du haschisch", comparing the effects of the two intoxicants, in *Le Messager de l'Assemblée* in 1851, immediately before his first substantial collection of poems, entitled "Les Limbes", appeared in the same periodical.

The extent to which Baudelaire was himself an addict, and whether his primary addiction was to alcohol or opium, is a matter of conjecture, but he was certainly fascinated by intoxication as a means of cultivating altered states of consciousness. He adopted a quasi-scientific viewpoint in researching the effects of various intoxicants, because cataloguing their effects seemed a necessary prelude to an evaluation of the exact extent and manner to which they might serve as a source or stimulus to literary creativity: a wellspring of inspiration. In reporting his results to the public, however,

Baudelaire represented his work in a subtly different manner, as a carefully-informed warning; "La poème de haschisch" ends with a formal "Morale," and when he was invited to talk about the subject-matter of his book in Brussels in 1864 he said forthrightly: "I wanted to write a book not of pure physiology, but above all of morality. I wanted to prove that seekers of paradise make their own hell, prepare it and hollow it out, with a success whose anticipation probably frightens them." Some readers have presumably taken this declared intention at face value, but a closer examination of the text and its context encourages a markedly different lesson.

Baudelaire's commentary on the effects of hashish is as dependent on second-hand experience as his commentary on opium, his description of the drug's effects being derived from Théophile Gautier's essay on "Hashish", which had first appeared in *La Presse* in 1843. (Different writers made their own choices as to how the borrowed word ought to be spelled in French.) Gautier, whose preface in the first posthumous reissue of *Les Fleurs du mal* established Baudelaire as the paradigm exemplar of the Decadent style, said in that essay that he had first met Baudelaire in 1849, but his memory must have been faulty, because he also indicated that Baudelaire had been present at some of the sessions of the "Club de Hachichins": meetings at the Hôtel Pimodan in the early 1840s, in which Gautier and other volunteers took that and other drugs supplied by and under the supervision of a physician named Joseph Moreau, who went on to publish a lengthy study of the effects of hashish on "mental alienation".

The sessions at the Hôtel Pimodan were not the first such collaboration between scientists and literary men. The English botanist Joseph Banks, who was the president of the Royal Society, the founder of the Royal Botanical Gardens at Kew and a key sponsor of exploratory expeditions to the far-flung corners of the globe, passed on exotic hallucinogens that his expeditionaries had gathered to Samuel Taylor Coleridge and his fellow Romantic poets, in order that their effects might be sampled (the chemist Humphry Davy did the same when he first discovered nitrous oxide, alias "laughing gas"). Just as Baudelaire's account of the effects of opium drew on

De Quincey, so De Quincey's drew on Coleridge, whose experiences became a benchmark for his own.

According to Gautier, Baudelaire only came to the Hôtel Pimodan as a spectator, although he had probably sampled hashish and opium during the abortive eastward journey he had taken in 1841 at the behest of his stepfather (who wanted to protect him from the ruinous effects of Parisian life). Although he had never reached his intended destination (Calcutta), Baudelaire had spent some months on the Île de France (Mauritius), where he would have had abundant opportunity to take both drugs, and to witness the effects of their long use. It would not be surprising if he had come to the uncompromising conclusions he reached in "Du vin et du haschisch"—that intoxicant drugs flatter the creative writer only to deceive, promising inspiration but ultimately suppressing and obliterating the ability to write—had he only had his own experiences to draw upon. Nor is it surprising, though, that he found much in De Quincey to support and re-emphasize that conclusion, as well as to confuse and complicate it, when he reiterated it in *Les Paradis artificiels*. The more important emphasis of the latter work is, however, a significant extension of the fundamental moral argument—and it is because of that extension that Baudelaire's appropriations from De Quincey made a highly significant contribution to the development of the Decadent world-view.

Like *Les Paradis artificiels, Confessions of an Opium Eater* poses as a moral tract—as it had to do in an England that was moving inexorably towards the rigidity of Victorianism, lest its readers might suspect it of the scandal of encouraging bad habits. De Quincey's preliminary address "from the author to the reader" is careful to promise the latter that the reward of reading the whole essay will be found in its eventual *moral* (the italicization is the author's). This protestation has as much to do with the fact that autobiography was still a dubious literary genre as with the particular subject-matter of the autobiographical essay in question; all writers of "confessions" tended to defend themselves against accusations of vainglory and narcissism by presenting their work in the guise of "spiritual autobiography".

"Spiritual autobiographers" excused the self-indulgence and implicit egotism of talking about themselves by formulating their life-stories as exemplary exercises in education, by means of which their catalogues of experience became training programs in moral enlightenment. It does not require unusual cynicism to judge all such processes of narrativization blatantly false—all the more so when they are ingenuous exercises in ludicrous self-delusion rather than instances of calculated hypocrisy. By the time that De Quincey wrote his *Confessions*, however, the pretence was no longer maintained as anything but a tokenistic show by anyone who could apply a grain of intelligence to their self-analysis—and De Quincey had far more than a grain to draw upon.

Earlier exercises in spiritual autobiography, and the literary parodies thereof that played such an important role in the early evolution of the novel, were probably less significant to De Quincey as material influences than more recently-fashionable modes of quasi-confessional writing, including the school of writing known as "graveyard poetry", whose paradigmatic exemplar was Edward Young's *Night Thoughts* (1742-45). His most important exemplar was undoubtedly Robert Burton's *The Anatomy of Melancholy* (1621), whose late-eighteenth-century reprint became a key taproot-text of English Romanticism. *The Anatomy of Melancholy* can be regarded as the work that pioneered the hybrid literary genre to which both *Confessions of an Opium Eater* and *Les Paradis artificiels* belong, artfully combining quasi-scientific observation of an unusual mental state with elaborate reflections on its relationship with personal artistic creativity.

Like Burton and Young, De Quincey and Baudelaire were intensely interested in the more tenebrous reaches of the human emotional spectrum. Although they are not identical, there is an obvious kinship between the anatomy and physiology of Burton's "melancholy" and Baudelaire's "spleen", within whose orbit Young's and De Quincey's ruminations operate. De Quincey's attempt to describe and define the transfiguration brought about by the continued use of opium represents it as a movement away from the quotidian manifestations of pain and ennui into what seems at first to be a far brighter and more energetic state of being, but whose trajectory eventually brings it back to something more closely akin to, but even more exasperated than, its starting-point.

De Quincey's account of "The Pleasures of Opium" never attains anything much resembling enthusiasm, and it is obvious to the reader from he start that it must be a prelude to a more substantial and thoughtful study of "The Pains of Opium". The latter are represented as an inevitable consequence of the former, and the result of an unavoidable process of evolution. De Quincey describes the critical point in this process in terms of a transfiguration of the quality of his dreams: "a theatre seemed suddenly opened and lighted up within my brain, which presented, nightly, spectacles of more than earthly splendour". He moves swiftly on to analyze the quality of this transfiguration in terms of four particular consequences:

> "1. That as the creative state of the eye increased, a sympathy seemed to arise between the waking and sleeping states of the brain in one point—that whatsoever I happened to call up and to trace by a voluntary act upon the darkness was very apt to transfer itself to my dreams; so that I feared to exercise this faculty; for, as Midas turned all things to gold, that yet baffled his hopes and defrauded his human desires, so whatsoever things capable of being visually represented I did but think of in the darkness, immediately shaped themselves into phantoms of the eye; and, by a process apparently no less inevitable, when thus once traced in faint and visionary colours, like writings in sympathetic ink, they were drawn out, by the fierce chemistry of my dreams, into insufferable splendour that fretted my heart.
>
> "2. For this, and all other changes in my dreams, were accompanied by deep-seated anxiety and gloomy melancholy, such as are wholly incommunicable by words. I seemed every night to descend—not metaphorically, but literally to descend—into chasms and sunless abysses, depths below depths, from which it seemed hopeless that I could ever reascend.

Nor did I, by waking, feel that I *had* reascended. This I do not dwell upon; because the state of gloom which attended these gorgeous spectacles, amounting at least to utter darkness, as of some suicidal despondency, cannot be approached by words.

"3. The sense of space, and in the end the sense of time, were both powerfully affected. Buildings, landscapes, etc., were exhibited in proportions so vast as the bodily eye is not fitted to receive. Space swelled, and was amplified to an extent of unutterable infinity. This, however, did not disturb me so much as the vast expansion of time: I sometimes seemed to have lived for 70 or 100 years in one night; nay, sometimes had feelings representative of a millennium passed in that time, or, however, of a duration far beyond the limits of any human experience."

The fourth point, which describes the effect that opium has on the workings of memory, is too long to quote in full here, but its conclusion is that nothing is ever entirely forgotten, and that no matter what veils are employed by the conscious mind to hide painful memories away, they can always be stripped away by the drug to reveal the memories in awful clarity.

In this description one can find the exaggerated essence of the aesthetic response that Edmund Burke had characterized as "the sublime", and the roots of the school of supernatural fiction devoted to the cultivation of what H. P. Lovecraft called "cosmic horror". Within the context of the present essay, however, its importance is the insistence that, no matter how discomfiting these sensations may be, they nevertheless allow access to a form of consciousness that is both more powerful and more accurate than quotidian consciousness, and which therefore exposes the artificiality of everyday life to the glare of a uniquely cold and callous illumination.

The introduction to the published fragments of *Suspiria de Profundis* [Sighs from the Depths] mentions a relapse into addiction suffered after publication of the first essay, which De Quincey describes as a "third prostration before the dark idol". The analysis cited in the first essay is taken for granted in the latter work, which was to have consisted of a collection of rhapsodic essays, including reportage of opium-dreams, discussing and illustrating the power of suffering to develop the human intellect. The best-known of these essays is "Levana and Our Ladies of Sorrow", which supplements the Roman goddess of childbirth, Levana, with a trinity of three "mother goddesses", named as Mater Lachrymarum [Our Lady of Tears], Mater Suspiriorum [Our Lady of Sighs] and Mater Tenebrarum [Our Lady of Darkness]. This trinity has exercised a powerful influence on the imagination of many subsequent writers, who have tended to detach them—as Baudelaire does—from their anchorage to Levana, and hence to the experience of childbirth.

Baudelaire was not only fascinated by the substance of these visions but also by the innovative manner of their expression. The lyrical fashion in which De Quincey describes the material of his visions established the fragments of *Suspiria de Profundis* as key examples of English poetry in prose; it is a great pity that the whole work—which was to have had thirty-two sections—was never completed, and that some of the records he made of his dreams were accidentally burned. The *Blackwood's* fragments were a significant influence on Baudelaire's work in the genre of prose poetry—a genre that Joris-Karl Huysmans regarded as the very essence of Decadent style. The final paragraph of Baudelaire's report attempts an analysis of the relationship of the published fragments of *Suspiria de Profundis* with personalized Death, and finds therein a symbolic summary and culmination of his own argument regarding the road to Hell mapped out by opium and other visionary stimulants.

De Quincey and Baudelaire both made conscientious attempts to ensure that their studies of altered states of consciousness could be construed as awful warnings, whose *raison d'être* is contained in their climactic moral admonitions by readers so disposed. In one respect, at least, they were perfectly honest, both concluding that habitual use of cannabis and/or opium have a severely depressive effect on the ability to write, in both the physical and psychological senses. In terms of the subject-matter of the visions and insights provided, however, they were considerably more ambivalent.

Even if there were not good reasons to suspect some deliberate hypocrisy in the moralistic poses adopted by De Quincey and Baudelaire, the larger pattern of each man's work offers clear proof of the fact that "prostration before the dark idol" is a much more profound matter than mere addictive compulsion. The heart of the underlying discourse of their essays is the conviction that, no matter how perversely self-destructive or implicitly evil such prostration might be, it nevertheless gives access to a kind of consciousness that is—in a terminology even stronger than Burke's—sublime.

Burke had argued in his account of the *Origins of our Ideas of the Sublime and the Beautiful* (1757) that there is always an element of horror in human contemplation in such archetypally sublime phenomena as the wild majesty of untamed nature and the vastness of the cosmos revealed by telescopes, but he had regarded the horror as a kind of seasoning. De Quincey moved the element of horror much closer to the center of his first account of the results of extended traffic with laudanum, and the 1845 essay credits it with a languorous and unrepentant voluptuousness far more explicit than anything in Burton, which had no significant precedent in English literature, with the possible exception of the English translation of William Beckford's *Vathek* (1787).

Baudelaire took the centrality of the horrific component of visionary experience for granted; the diplomacy he exercised in *Les Paradis artificiels* and his commentaries thereon was largely set aside in his poetic celebrations of the inevitable and deliberate extension of ennui into spleen. In one of the longest poems in *Les Fleurs du mal*, "Le Voyage" (first published in the *Revue Française*, 10 April 1859), Baudelaire waxed lyrical upon this aspect of the artist's journey; its seventh section begins with the lines:

> Amer savoir, celui qu'on tire du voyage!
> Le monde, monotone et petit, aujourd'hui,
> Hier, demain, toujours, nous fait voir image:
> Une oasis d'horreur dans un désert d'ennui!

(A bitter truth is that which draws the voyager on! The world, monotonous and petty today, yesterday, tomorrow and forever, makes us see ourselves as an oasis of horror in a desert of ennui!)

The ironic representation of horror as an oasis in a desert puts a different spin on the statement Baudelaire made in his 1864 lecture, to the effect that "seekers of paradise make their own hell, prepare it and hollow it out, with a success whose anticipation probably frightens them". He is not issuing an orthodox Christian warning against temptation, instructing his fellow artists to forsake the Devil and all his works; the subtext of what he saying is, in fact, that once we have accepted that there is no paradise, we had best try to appreciate the rewards of its opposite and be as grateful as we can, in spite of anticipatory dread and eventual pain, for the kind of enlightenment that visionary experience can and does provide.

This conclusion had, of course, been implicit in Thomas De Quincey's four-part list of the torments that opium brings, and extravagantly symbolized by his account of the spiritual anatomy of the holy trinity of Our Ladies of Sorrow. It is, De Quincey asserted, a direly discomfiting trial by ordeal to find one's dreams and waking thoughts overlapping and merging, with the result that the latter are corrupted by the former, to find one's dreams falling perpetual prey to "gloom and anxiety", to experience the authentic and overwhelming vastness of space and time, and to discover that the most carefully-hidden memories can still break through their multitudinous veils—but all of those discoveries are, indeed, *discoveries*: phantoms whose undeniable testimony is that "real experience" is a tissue of contrivances, and that the noumenal reality behind the world of phenomena is inherently horrific to the rapt human mind. (De Quincey makes considerable reference in the *Confessions* to the philosophy of Immanuel Kant, and is entirely likely to have thought of his revelations in these Kantian terms).

De Quincey concludes his first essay not with dutiful cries of lamentation—although there is certainly a note of woe about its exceedingly long final paragraph—but with the offer of leaving his body to science, if there be a man of science who thinks that their might be anything to be learned from its dissection, That was a shocking proposal in its era, psychologically akin to the kinds of martyrdom recorded in the *Golden Legend*. Although one could hardly describe the gesture as a thirsty man's view of an oasis, it exhibits a kind of stubborn pride in damnation that prepared the way for the more elaborate dalliance with darkness, grief and sorrow expressed in the dream-summaries contained in the *Suspiria*.

Even in De Quincey's first essay, the horror of visionary experience is counted on the credit side rather than the debit, and the final analysis re-emphasizes that manner of calculation. Baudelaire followed the same pattern more extravagantly, especially in the way that he developed visionary imagery in his poetry, giving full voice to the perverse voluptuousness of horror, thus paving the way not merely for the Decadent Movements of the *fin-de-siècle* but for the twentieth-century development of such subgenres as comic horror fiction. "Le Voyage" is the direct ancestor of a chain of visionary odysseys whose landmark works include Oscar Wilde's "The Sphinx" (1874), George Sterling's "A Wine of Wizardry" (1907) and Clark Ashton Smith's "The Hashish-Eater; or, The Apocalypse of Evil" (1922). What those any kindred works develop is a sensibility in which the experience of horror is not to be shunned, nor allowed to provoke a reflexive reaction of revulsion, but is rather something to be savored, not as a spice but as the main course of the imaginary meal.

The modern reader, considering Gautier's account of the effects of hashish and De Quincey's account of the effects of a cocktail of morphine and alcohol in the context of a much more elaborate scientific literature, will realize immediately that the texture of their experiences owed far less to the physiological effects of the drugs than to the power of their own imagination and their genius for improvisation. Most seekers after cosmic truth by this route have, inevitably, found nothing but reflections of their own stupidity.

The modern reader will also be well aware that the scientific method proved perfectly adequate to the revelation of the true extent of the scales of space and time appropriate to the imaginative contemplation of the universe, and far stranger extremes of sublimity—and will, in consequence, be in no doubt as to the significance of the essential element of horror contained in the scientific revelation.

De Quincey's intuition was a product of its time, just as the Decadent Movements were, and there is a naivety in their delight that we can only consume nostalgically. By the same token, however, there is an essential modernity in their anticipations, an incontrovertible accuracy in their brilliance, to which we ought to pay due homage. It is arguable that De Quincey exhibited even more prophetic acumen elsewhere—in his essay on "Murder Considered as One of the Fine Arts", for example—and he was not the first observer to take note of the fact that the human mind finds reality a difficult thing to bear, but it was in *Confessions of an Opium Eater* and *Suspiria de Profundis* that he discovered the utility of the Decadent style and its key form in expressing that sensibility. Those two essays brought the genre of spiritual autobiography to the limit of its own decadence, and injected it with a new kind of dishonesty, less hypocritical and far healthier than any that had gone before, thus laying vital groundwork for Baudelaire to take the sublime sensibility in question to greater heights of expression.

## IV.

## THE QUEEN OF DENIAL

The idea of cultural decadence was by no means new when Charles-Louis le Secondat, Baron de La Brède et de Montesquieu, published his *Considérations sur les causes de la grandeur des Romains et de leur décadence* in 1734. The idea that the glories of imperial Rome had given way to the Dark Ages because its rulers had embraced debauchery rather than cultivating ambition was commonplace even while the process was in train, and the Romans who complained of it had their own conspicuous historical precedent on which to look back: the fate of the empire built by Alexander the Great, whose ruins the Rome of Caesar and Augustus had usurped. Indeed, the prophets of doom that Rome produced in such awesome profusion began crying "Woe!" even as Rome acquired the peak of its achievement in the Augustan era. Their successors, meditating upon this prophecy fulfilled, suggested that the seeds of decadence had been planted while imperial Rome was still in the process of its birth, the most obvious of those seeds of infection being a woman, whose name was Cleopatra.

The Roman historians were well aware of the fact that the empire that preceded their own had itself consumed the ruins of an earlier magnificence: the kingdom of Egypt, whose proudest and most powerful pharaohs had built the pyramids. So significant was this annexation that it was on Egypt's shore that Alexander the Great established the city named after him, host to the great library that was the very heart of Classical cultural achievement. Having conquered Egypt, whose Nile-watered plain was then the most fertile and fecund land in the Mediterranean, the Greeks had installed their own pharaonic dynasty, which had adopted many of the attitudes and customs of the lineage they had replaced—including the practice of royal incest, to prevent dilution of their bloodline—and had in consequence become an emblem of decadence redoubled in Roman eyes. When Julius Caesar began an liaison with the Queen of Egypt, having deposed her brother in her favor, the scandal cut far deeper than any commonplace adultery, and when Caesar's avenger Mark Antony deserted his own intended bride—the sister of Octavian, who was later to rename himself Augustus—for the same temptress, she must have seemed to many Romans to be a veritable succubus, intent on stealing and degrading the virility of the embryonic empire.

The importance of Montesquieu's analysis of Roman decadence was not that its fundamental contention was new or controversial; its originality lay in the nature of its explanation. Montesquieu was a historian in search of patterns, who sought to make a science out of his discipline by discovering generalizations and formulating theories as to their causes. Montesquieu refused to see the disintegration of the Roman Empire as a concatenation of idiosyncratic accidents; he represented it instead as the unfolding of a destiny, whose form had already been foreshadowed in the fates of Egypt and Greece, which found a ready analogy in the life-cycle of human individuals. In Montesquieu's view, empires grew old just as humans did, first losing their virility and then becoming senile.

Montesquieu's contention that there was an underlying logic to the fate of Rome implied that some such pattern would be discoverable in the fates of other past empires, whose rises and falls were then becoming more clearly discernible to European scholarship: empires in India, China and South America .It implied, too, that the same fate would eventually overtake any aspirant empire currently in the building, including those nurtured by the contemporary European superpowers: England, Holland and France. More than that: the example of Rome implied that each of these embryonic empires was likely to carry within its evolving body politic the discernible seeds of its own destruction: omens not merely legible but conspicuous to those capable of interpreting them.

Théophile Gautier undoubtedly had Montesquieu's thesis in mind when he wrote his introduction to the third edition of Charles Baudelaire's *Les Fleurs du Mal*, in which he issued his famous definition of decadent style: "Art arrived at that point of extreme maturity that determines civilizations which have grown old; ingenious, complicated, clever, full of delicate hints and refinements, gathering all the delicacies of speech, borrowing from technical vocabularies, taking colour from every palette, tones from all musical instruments, contours vague and fleeting, listening to translate subtle confidences, confessions of depraved passions and the odd hallucinations of a fixed idea turning to madness".

Had this passage not been published as an introduction to Baudelaire, no contemporary French reader would have take it as anything other than a description of Gautier's own work. He goes on to talk of the application of this style "ventur[ing] to the very extremes" of "language already veined with the greenness of decomposition...[in] the necessary and fatal idiom of peoples and civilizations where an artificial life has replaced a natural one." This methodology does, indeed, echo in much of Baudelaire's work, but it *is* an echo, albeit one that is carefully refined and replenished. Baudelaire's own contribution to the Decadent style was to apply it in the manner of a "painter of modern life" and not as an antiquarian or a student of exotica. Its application to the contemplation of the Classical past had already been explored by a number of writers, including such Parnassian poets as Charles Leconte de Lisle and Theodore de Banville; in prose, it had not merely been done but spectacularly overdone by Gautier himself, most obviously and most notably in a series of historical novellas that reconstructed images of life in Classical times as a series of philosophical parables inspired by Montesquieu's thesis. The first item in that series, which remained the most spectacular, was "Une nuit de Cléopâtre" (1838).

"Une nuit de Cléopâtre" is best-known in English as the headpiece of a classic collection of stories translated and assembled by Lafcadio Hearn, who was then the foremost American exponent of decadent style: *One of Cleopatra's Nights and Other Fantastic Romances* (Worthington, 1882). Hearn's collection also contains versions of two similar historical romances featuring fabulous temptreses: "Le roi Candaule" (1844; tr. as "King Candaules") and "Arria Marcella: souvenir de Pompeii" (1852; the tr. omits the subtitle). The latter is a timeslip fantasy, in which a contemporary Frenchman is drawn out of his own environment into a world of pure glamour by the eponymous courtesan, who is now posthumously active as a kind of succubus or lamia. In the conclusion of the story, borrowed from an episode in the fanciful *Life of Apollonius of Tyana* compiled by Philostratus, the supernatural predator is exposed and her spell broken, but the hero's release can only return him to a life of regret and disappointment—a pattern previously played out, in even more feverish fashion, in the seminal vampire story "La morte amoureuse" (1836; tr. as "Clarimonde"). Further versions of the same plot are more playfully featured in the shorter translations included in the Hearn collection: "Omphale" (1834; the tr. is subtitled "A Rococo Story") and "Le pied de la Momie" (1840; tr. as "The Mummy's Foot").

Viewed as a set of variants on a theme, Hearn's collection of translations is a definitive contribution to the Romantic myth of the *femme fatale*: the exotic lover whose magical allure far exceeds any fascination that any mundane sexual partner could ever induce. Hearn's selection of his title-piece is, however, as clever as it is significant. because it recognizes Cleopatra as Gautier's archetype of the species: the ultimate *femme fatale* (a role in which other writers had preferred and would prefer to cast such figures as Lilith, Salome and Circe). For Gautier, Cleopatra is the archetypal succubus not because she was more beautiful, or more famous, than Arria Marcella or Nyssia (Candaules' wife), but because she was the centre-piece of Montesquieu's analysis of the omens that had spelled out the Roman Empire's demise in advance. She was the perfect embodiment, not merely of the decadent lifestyle, but of the premonition of decadence. She is no mere enchantress but an inexorable force of nature: the germ of a decadence whose symptoms have yet to come into bloom, but whose fatality is already established.

Gautier begins his story with an assertion that the story took place 1,900 years before the time of its writing—a figure far from exact, given that it cannot be set any earlier than 37 B.C., 1,875 years before 1838, but which serves to emphasize an implication of historical symmetry. The narrative commences with a careful description of Cleopatra's barge moves down the Nile in stately fashion, impelled by fifty oarsmen. She is returning from the celebration of a religious rite at a shrine at Hermonthis (a city upriver of Thebes), and she is suffering from the desperate kind of boredom that is dignified even in English by the name of ennui. She describes this state of mind in great detail to her devoted slave Charmion, explaining how the deserts, temples and religion of Egypt combine to produce it. She laments, too, that a queen can never know whether she is loved for herself or for her crown.

The author then introduces Meïamoun, an extraordinarily handsome youth who has been following the barge for some while. Like the queen, who is a descendant of the Ptolemys, his ancestry is Greek. His infatuation with the beautiful Cleopatra is every bit as desperate, and just as perverse, as her ennui. Cleopatra catches a glimpse of the swimming Meïamoun from her palace, but has no inkling of his purpose, which is to fire an arrow into her room bearing an unsigned scroll declaring his love. Meïamoun hides in the palace grounds, in the hope of obtaining a glimpse of Cleopatra while she is bathing, and succeeds in so doing—but she catches sight of him again, and he is seized by her attending eunuchs. When he identifies himself as the sender of the scroll Cleopatra decides that she will make his dreams of love come true for a single night, after which he must die. He readily consents.

By way of foreplay, Cleopatra and Meïamoun share a munificent banquet and watch voluptuous dances, which reach their climax when the queen takes the floor herself. When daybreak eventually arrives, Meïamoun moves to take the cup of poison that he has agreed to drink. The queen reaches out momentarily to prevent him, but then hears the sound of trumpets announcing the approach of Mark Antony, after which she allows him to complete his suicide. Cleopatra condescends to shed a single tear upon the body of her dead lover—the only one she ever let fall, according to the narrative voice—but is ready immediately thereafter to meet her Roman consort with a charming smile and a casual explanation of the presence of the corpse.

The sixth and final chapter of the *nouvelle* begins with the contention that the banquets, orgies and other assorted delights of the modern world are very meager by comparison with those of the world of antiquity. This is probably untrue, but it is an essential element in the gaudy image of antiquity that Gautier is trying to construct. The contrast he is drawing is not between a world reveling in the fatality of its decay and a world whose progress is unstoppable, but between a world whose decadence was blithely glorious and a world whose drab materialism reflects an absurd unconsciousness of its inevitable decline.

The reader of the story is, of course, expected to know—vaguely, at least—what happened to Antony and Cleopatra after its conclusion. Like Meïamoun, Mark Antony is also destined to die, ostensibly for love of Cleopatra. Cynical historians, however, tend to the view that he married her for her money—which financed his Parthian campaign—rather than her beauty. The marriage caused him a great deal of trouble in Rome, but he probably had the example of his mentor Caesar in mind, who also had to go to dubious extremes to obtain the money to finance the Gallics Wars, but reaped spectacular rewards when he returned triumphant. In the event, he merely provided Octavian with an invaluable pretext to attack him. Even then, Antony might have won the naval battle of Actium—and perhaps returned to power in Rome—had he and Cleopatra been able to agree on and adhere to a common strategy; when the critical moment of the conflict arrived, however, the two of them did not act in unison.

Given all this, it is understandable that Gautier feels justified in assuring the reader that Cleopatra will not be shedding any tears for Mark Antony. He feels fully entitled to assume that the single night with Meïamoun that he invented—which must take place when she is in her thirties—would have provide a fitting climax for Cleopatra's rich and varied career as a lover, just as it provides a fitting climax for Meïamoun's narrower erotic experience. In making this point, it is perhaps worth noting that Hearn's translation of Gautier's title—retained by F. C. Sumichrast in his subsequent edition of *The Works of Théophile Gautier* (1900-03)—is not exact. Although it would be equally misleading to translate Gautier's title as "A Night with Cleopatra," the implication of the title is clearly that "One Night of Cleopatra" would exceed the reward of a much more varied and extended love-life of a more mundane stripe, rather than the suggestion that Meïamoun was merely one among many "nights" of similar inconsequentiality. It is significant that Meïamoun, like Cleopatra and the city of Alexandria, is a relic of the empire of Alexander the Great; she and he are "made for one another" in a way that she and Mark Antony are not.

The fact that Cleopatra's love-affair with Meïamoun lasts but a single night does not lessen its perfection; indeed, it secures it. Its brevity leaves no space for even the deflating erosion of excitement that is conventionally dignified by its French term—post-coital *triste*—let alone for the dwindling of interest and involvement that afflicts Cleopatra's marriage to Mark Antony. There is, therefore, a sense in which Meïamoun's aspirations and protestations of love are not as absurd as they might seem. They may have started out as perverse optimism, but the single tear that Cleopatra sheds put them in a new light retrospectively. What, after all, has Meïamoun suffered for Cleopatra's sake? He has avoided old age and the waning of virility; he has avoided the living decay of body and mind into senility and incontinence. He has, in brief, avoided the fate of Rome—a fate that could not possibly have been avoided in any other way.

The ending of "Une nuit de Cléopâtre" stands in striking contrast to the endings of "La morte amoureuse" and "Arria Marcella," in both of which the male lovers are forced to live on, awaiting death in a state of utter spiritual desolation. It contrasts, too, with the ending of "Le roi Candaule," in which the king who unwisely allows his friend Gyges to see his alluring wife naked is punished for his recklessness by assassination and replacement. The latter ending may seem "happier" by modern standards, if one sides with the temptation-maddened Gyges, but it is not; Gyges merely becomes Candaules, afflicted by the same anxieties that drive his predecessor to distraction, compelled by experience to resist their relief. The protagonists of "Omphale" and "Le pied de la Momie" get away more lightly, by virtue of not taking their erotic experiences too seriously, but there is a sense in which that very inability is their tragedy. In a game that no one can win, Meïamoun is, at the end of the day, the one who loses least.

The ennui that plagues Gautier's Cleopatra was to become the central motif of Decadent literature, although it was extrapolated by Baudelaire into its more ardently-inflamed augmentation, spleen. Cleopatra's account of it is idiosyncratically interesting by virtue of the manner in which it extends a chain of metaphors likening her mental state to the physical and cultural state of Egypt. Her inability to reach the state of emotional arousal that would permit her to shed tears is likened to the aridity of the desert; the oppression of her spirit is symbolized by the colossal temples and tombs, and by the haunting ever-presence of animal-headed gods and guardian sphinxes; her awareness of her own mortality—the angst that threatens to make all human experience seem worthless—is accentuated by her sense of being surrounded by the innumerable mummies of past generations, uncannily preserved. How, she wonders, can a creature like her—a natural devotee of laughter and merriment—possibly overcome such sinister influences? She cannot; her nature is not her own to dictate. She is a helpless prisoner of history, who must play her role as Queen of Egypt and seed of decay. Given all that, she has ample reason to be grateful to Meïamoun, who enlivens her soul for a precious instant, and reduces her to the expression of a mere sentiment.

Modern literary criticism tends to be suspicious of the stylistic excesses of such works as "Une nuit de Cléopâtre" and Hearn's version of "One of Cleopatra's Nights"; as extravagant exercises in what is nowadays often dismissed as "purple prose" they are unparalleled. The decadent style is, however, the only one that could possibly be employed to create and sustain the mood of such a parable. Modern erotic fantasies that still insist on representing love as if it were a kind of supernatural force, whose experience is the greatest possible exaltation of human feeling, rarely attempt to dress their rhetoric as vividly as Gautier and Hearn, not because their authors no longer think infatuation a fit topic for extravagant celebration, but because they can only see it as a matter of individual eccentricity. In Cleopatra's case, it is more than that; just as her ennui was the reflection of an extinct empire occupied by another whose extinction is still in bud, so its momentary interruption is a *bouleversement* of the historical pattern, a blow struck against the march of time.

It is, of course, an ultimately futile blow in Gautier's and Montesquieu's way of thinking—if history is subject to natural laws, they cannot be defied, any more than the mortality of the individual can be denied—but that does not mean that the blow should not and need not be struck. On the contrary; it should and must, if that is the only expression of human power, the only manifestation of human pride, and the only result of human artifice that history can tolerate. It is a mistake to think of Gautier's calculatedly ornate prose as something garish and false; even though this Egypt and this Cleopatra never existed outside the literary imagination, they are authentic in a sense that really does matter—far more authentic, in encapsulating a particular idea of the world, than the actuality of a night of Cleopatra's favors could ever have been in reality.

Three years before he wrote "Une nuit de Cléopâtre" Gautier had penned another lushly erotic fantasy in *Mademoiselle de Maupin* (1835), which had carried an introduction to which his introduction to *Le Fleurs du Mal* might be considered a sequel. The introduction to Mademoiselle de Maupin is the manifesto of the doctrine of *"l'art pour l'art"*, a phrase usually rendered into English as "art for art's sake", which was to become the motto of the English Decadent Movement by courtesy of Oscar Wilde's fervent advocacy. "Une nuit de Cléopâtre" is a cardinal example of *"l'art pour l'art"*, not in the false sense that it has no moral or didactic purpose—all literary works are morally ordered and didactically effective, because they cannot avoid that destiny—but in the true sense that it is a work of art that advocates artifice and artistry, and celebrates their triumph, even in a world when they can escape impotence only momentarily. The alternative, as the story makes clear, is never to escape it at all—and who one earth would prefer that?

Although the central figure of *Mademoiselle de Maupin* is the eponymous heroine, flitting from disguise to disguise, there is one remarkable passage in the book devoted entirely to the state of mind of the hero, d'Albert, which maps out the hectic and seemingly perverse pattern of his desires once he has fallen in love with "Théodore," whom he falsely believes to be a man. The model takes the form of a "theater" whose apparatus and orchestra are made up of insects, while the souls of poets are accommodated in its mother-of-pearl stalls, using dewdrops as opera-glasses. The scenery is utterly exotic, the sky being striped, and the players wear the most fantastic costumes imaginable. The characters depicted there are not from any known place or period of history, nor do their actions display any comprehensible motives; the plots through which they move defy causality, and their dialogue is chaotic. This extended description of a world turned upside down dissolves into a supplementary vision, in which d'Albert represents his soul as an equally fabulous continent, lush and splendid but fatally haunted by decay. Although these flights of the imagination are prompted in the narrative by a scheme to mount a production of Shakespeare's *As You Like It*, a play whose plot hinges on mistakes caused by the characters cross-dressing, thus constituting a metaphorical depiction of sexual confusion, they are also a further cardinal example of "*l'art pour l'art*" and a passionate advocacy of artifice and artistry in its purest sense: as a gallant defiance of "natural law," which flies in the face of impotence.

Gautier returned to the theme of supernatural infatuation once more after "Arria Marcella," in *Spirite; nouvelle fantastique* (1866), most of whose translations retain the same title. Unlike his earlier accounts of *femmes fatales*, this is a sentimental fantasy, earnestly describing a love affair between a young man and a female ghost. It was written for the ballet-dancer Carlotta Grisi, for whom Gautier also wrote the libretto of the ballet *Giselle*. It was, in fact, Carlotta's sister Ernesta who actually lived with Gautier and bore him two daughters, but Gautier insisted on regarding Carlotta as the one true love of his life, and defiantly provided *Spirite* with the only kind of happy ending that seemed practicable in the circumstances: the lovers are eventually united, but in death rather than life. His Cleopatra might well have been scornful of such a device, considering one moment of living ecstasy infinitely more valuable than an eternity of disembodied companionship, but she would probably have understood the appeal of the fantasy.

In the kind of death that the protagonists of *Spirite* achieve there is no empire, no decay, no ennui and no natural law; there is nothing to resist, and hence no artistry, no artifice, nor any cause to shed a tear. It is, in its own strange way, seductive—but again, who on earth could prefer it to the bolder and quintessentially regal kind of denial represented in "Une nuit de Cléopâtre"?

# V.

## DANDYISM AND THE SPLENDOR AND MISERY OF COURTESANS

Charles Baudelaire summarized his opinions on the theory and practice of dandyism—the lifestyle fantasy aspect of the idealized masculine Decadent pose—in *Le peintre de la moderne vie* (tr. as "The Painter of Modern Life"), written in 1861 and published in 1863. Disguised as an essay in art criticism, inspired by the work of an artist unnamed in the piece (actually Constantin Guys), *Le peintre de la moderne vie* is actually a compendium of Baudelaire's ideas on the aesthetics of modernity, as relevant to literature and lifestyle as to painting. The ninth section of the essay, "The Dandy", defines such an individual as a "man of wealth and leisure, who, even though weary of it, has no other occupation than the pursuit of pleasure [and] no other profession than that of elegance".

The author promptly confesses that true dandies are only found in novels, especially in love stories. He suggests that they are a vital component of literary love stories because "it is, unfortunately, quite true that, without leisure and money, love can be nothing but a plebeian orgy or the fulfillment of a conjugal duty". In novels featuring fabulously wealthy characters, Baudelaire points out, love is "a burning or a fantastical caprice" rather than the "loathsome utility" to which it usually has to be reduced in life. He strikes a cautionary note, however, by saying that, although love is "the natural occupation of the leisured", the dandy "does not make love his specific aim" any more than he wants "to have money for its own sake". He also dismisses the common mistake of considering dandyism to be "an immoderate interest in personal appearance and material elegance". For the true dandy, Baudelaire claims, these pursuits are merely symbols of "the aristocratic superiority of his personality"; dandyism is, above all, "a burning need to acquire originality within the apparent bounds of convention". It is "a sort of cult of oneself" dedicated to "the delight in causing astonishment, and the proud satisfaction of never being astonished oneself".

Dandies, according to Baudelaire, "all have the same characteristics of opposition and revolt" and they "represent the best element in human pride—that need, which nowadays is too uncommon, to combat and destroy triviality". Dandyism is, in sum, "the last gleam of heroism in times of decadence", as "superb, cold and melancholy" as a setting sun. Like Barbey d'Aurevilly before him, Baudelaire names the English "Regency Buck" George "Beau" Brummell as a model dandy, but recognizes that the authentic original of the model in question was Brummell's friend, Lord Byron, who had the personality to go with the appearance.

Baudelaire had toyed with the possibility of attempting a (necessarily partial) realization of the lifestyle fantasy of dandyism himself, before his mother and her second husband, General Aupick, severed his access to his inheritance and put him on an allowance, rightly concluding that he would squander the lot in no time if he were left to his own devices. However bitter he was about that restriction, Baudelaire had always known full well that no practical experiment in lifestyle fantasy could last long, and that any that he might have attempted could never have amounted to more than a shallow affectation. He was not, after all, a character in a novel, and he had read more than enough to know that conscientious novelists ran into difficulties when they undertook to tackle the thorny question of how an aspirant dandy was to obtain the effectively-unlimited funds he would need to play his part.

In particular, Baudelaire was familiar with the works of Honoré de Balzac, certain of which represent dandyism as a temporarily-viable lifestyle for handsome young men, provided that their own naïve scruples are compensated by the cynical unscrupulousness of older and wiser mentors. Balzac cannot qualify as a Decadent writer on the grounds of his literary style, which is conversational and earnest rather than decorative and ironic, and his world-view smacks of determined sentimentality in its attitude to the lives of ordinary folk, but when he turns his attention to the French aristocracy, Balzac is in no doubt whatsoever as to the advanced state of its innate moral and historical decay in the early nineteenth century. Indeed, none of the great Decadent novelists of the *fin de siècle* was as ruthlessly scathing in offering accounts of the decadence of contemporary aristocracy as Balzac had been, and none had his strangely lascivious appreciation of the corruption that is bound to be wrought in the soul of an outsider desirous of ascending into the *haut monde*—the dandy's natural habitat.

Within the sprawling tapestry of the *Comédie humaine* there are two characters, in particular, who exemplify Balzac's theory of aspirant dandyism. The better-known of the two is Eugène de Rastignac, whose story is told in one of the most popular individual texts in the series, *Le Père Goriot* (1835; tr. as *Old Goriot*), but the more revealing is Lucien Chardon, alias Lucien de Rubempré, whose biography is distributed in patchwork fashion within the longest story-sequence in the series, which was ultimately brought together in two volumes, *Les Illusions perdues* (tr. as *Lost Illusions*) and *Splendeurs et misères de courtesans* (tr. under various titles, including *The Splendors and Miseries of Courtesans*, but long better known in the prim UK as *A Harlot's Progress*). These two components of the series actually include seven distinct parts, whose dates of composition and original publication overlapped somewhat. The former brings together *Les Deux poètes* (1837; tr. as "Two Poets"), *Un Grand homme de province à Paris* (1839; tr. as "A Provincial Celebrity in Paris") and *Les Souffrances de l'inventeur* (1843; tr. as "The Sufferings of an Inventor"). The first portion of the second component was initially published as *La Torpille* (1838) before being reprinted in combination with the second section of the final version of the novel, "À combien l'amour revient aux vieillards" (tr. as "What Love Costs an Old Man") as *Esther, or Les amours d'un vieux banquier* (1843); in the final version it is retitled "Esther heureuse" (tr. as "Esther Happy"). The third and fourth parts of the second volume were separately published as *Ou mènent les mauvais chemins* (1846; tr. as "The End of Evil Ways" although "Where Bad Roads Lead" is arguably more accurate) and *La Dernière incarnation de Vautrin* (1847; tr. as "Vautrin's Last Avatar").

Balzac's two aspirant dandies are linked by virtue of the fact that both are offered Faustian bargains by a curious character whose real name is Jacques Collin, although he uses several others and is usually referred to as Vautrin, that being the pseudonym under which readers first make his acquaintance in *Le Père Goriot*. Whereas Rastignac refuses to make a pact with Collin, Lucien accepts his terms. The eventual result of these contrasted decisions is that Rastignac thrives and Lucien perishes, but any attempt to draw a moral from that distinction is deeply confused by the fact that Balzac had shifted his own viewpoint considerably between writing the first of the seven story-segments and the last—a change of mind and heart reflected in a drastic alteration of his characterization of the cynical and satanic puppet-master Jacques Collin.

Balzac's theory of dandyism is based on the assumption that all Parisian marriages are made for money, and that it is universally accepted that wealthy married women will support handsome lovers—or, more rarely, handsome husbands—in glorious idleness, just as their wealthy husbands will maintain young and pretty mistresses if they have not married trophy wives. These lovers and trophy husbands have to dress up to earn their money and are obliged to cultivate themselves as objects of worship for themselves and their devotees—but that, of course, is exactly what the dandy wants to do and be. Once Rastignac has determined to adopt the lifestyle of a dandy, for as long as he might be able to sustain it, he discovers two ways in which he might achieve it. The first involves seducing Delphine von Nucingen, the ungrateful daughter of the eponymous Père Goriot, while the second involves marrying Victorine Taillefer, a girl who is presently poor, but who will become a rich heiress if her brother happens to die—an eventuality that Vautrin volunteers to ensure, if Rastignac will promise to give him a substantial slice of the fortune he will acquire by the marriage. The ending of *Le Père Goriot* is a trifle vague regarding Rastignac's exact intentions, although it is very definite about his spirit of opposition and revolt, but subsequent works set at later dates confirm that Rastignac did indeed cling to his resolve to resist Vautrin's diabolical temptation—in spite of the fact that Vautrin does arrange the brother's murder, and the fact that Victorine loves him—and spurned the prospect of a potentially happy marriage in order to become Delphine's lover.

Lucien's story is much more complicated than Rastignac's. In *Les Deux poètes* his ambitions are purely literary, and he is ambitious to leave his provincial home for Paris because that is where literary reputations are made. In order to do that, however, he has to prostitute himself in the same fashion as Rastignac, using his extraordinary good looks to insinuate himself into the favor of Madame de Bargeton, who "elopes" with him to Paris, but is then persuaded by his insidious rival, Sixte du Châtelet, to drop him. The second narrative to be written, *La Torpille*, finds Lucien at a considerably later stage in his career, having been taken up by Jacques Collin and having formally accepted a bargain similar to the one that Rastignac turned down. Collin is working hard to secure Lucien a title and an extremely profitable marriage, but the situation is complicated by the fact that Lucien has fallen in love with a whore named Esther, whose nickname—which likens her to an electric eel—provides the novel's title. Collin has perforce to take Esther's career in hand too, sending her to a religious finishing school in order to refine her character. This pattern of complication was to be further extended and entangled in the next two parts of the story-sequence, when Collin attempts to finance Lucien's ascent by using Esther to milk the Baron von Nucingen—Delphine's exceedingly unpleasant husband—who has fallen in love with her on sight without knowing who she is.

Balzac soon followed *La Torpille* with the much longer novel *Un Grand homme de province à Paris,* which filled in a considerable section of Lucien's history prior to his fateful meeting with his mentor. It describes in great and heartfelt detail the vicissitudes that afflict Lucien following his abandonment by Madame de Bargeton, as he tries to make his way in Paris as a professional writer. He finds the Parisian literary marketplace utterly corrupt, and is seduced into the most corrupt of all its sectors—popular journalism—when a young actress named Coralie falls in love with him and he feels obliged to make an impression; it is at this point that his aspirations to dandyism are formulated. He turns out to have a talent for journalistic work, but his failure to comprehend the niceties of his precarious situation proves disastrous. Coralie is led by her infatuation to sever her ties with her rich protector, Camusot, and the necessity of financing their lifestyle brings Lucien inexorably to financial ruin. He is eventually led to forge promissory notes, which ruin his closest friend and brother-in-law—whose tragedy is recounted, in excruciating detail, in *Les Souffrances de l'inventeur*—and is about to commit suicide in consequence when he meets a supposed Spanish clergyman and diplomat, Carlos Herrera—actually Jacques Collin in another of his disguises—and is persuaded to return to Paris instead, with his ambition to become a true dandy revitalized. His literary pretensions are now forgotten.

Collin's grand plans are eventually thwarted, in *Ou mènent les mauvais chemins*, by a group of policemen who become his determined adversaries when Baron von Nucingen hires them to discover Esther's identity. He thwarts them more than once, but is eventually undone by an unfortunate combination of events following the suicide of poor Esther, who cannot bear to go on living once Lucien's acquisition of a title and a wife—which seem imminent and inevitable—will make it impossible for them to continue their torrid love-affair. Collin almost manages to solve the problem, but the examining magistrate assigned to the case happens to be the son of the Camusot from whom Lucien stole Coralie, and is eager to pay him back. The younger Camusot tricks Lucien into betraying Collin, quite unnecessarily, and when Lucien realizes what he has done he kills himself, almost breaking the heart of his current aristocratic mistress, Madame de Sérizy, as well as disappointing the wealthy spinster to whom Collin had intended to marry him.

Given that Lucien's suicide merely completes the intention he had formed before he first met Collin, it might be taken as a confirmation of the moral principle that no good can come of making deals with the Devil, but Balzac went on to add a fourth part to *Splendeurs et misères des courtisanes*, in which Collin promptly finds another young man to rescue from the guillotine, and then achieves a curious form of self-redemption by joining the police. Some critics feel that the volume compounded out of the four subsections would be better off without this fourth part, on the grounds that the story of Esther and Lucien concludes with their deaths, but this overlooks the fact that it is Collin, not the doomed lovers, who is—or, at least, becomes in the course of the narrative—the central character of the portmanteau text.

The stories of Rastignac and Lucien both confirm—and might perhaps have inspired—Baudelaire's assertion that although love is the natural pursuit of the leisured, it cannot be the focal point of the dandy's concern. Both stories assert, in no uncertain terms, that true love is a disaster for the would-be dandy. Rastignac's preference for Delphine over Victorine may seem incomprehensible to a modern reader, trained by a century of love stories to believe that a happy ending can only be achieved by preferring the saintly innocent to the heartless schemer—all the more so because he would not suffer financially by making the other choice—but it becomes comprehensible when one remembers that Rastignac's objective is not to attain a conventional "happy ending" but to gain entry into the *haut monde*, which lives by very different values. His aim is to be a dandy, an object of self-worship, entire unto himself; Victorine's true love could only be a handicap to him. In refusing to make a diabolical pact with Collin, therefore, he is not committing himself to the side of the angels, but simply preferring a different, and somewhat less vulgar, road to hell.

By the same token, although Lucien does accept Collin's offer of a pact, he is unable to follow it through. He is not fitted to be a dandy, although he is even better-looking than Rastignac, because he is too deeply steeped in provincial sentimentality. He is fatally vulnerable to the kind of love that manifests itself as a "burning and fantastical caprice" and fundamentally antithetical to the kind of "loathsome utility" that Collin cunningly forges from Esther's love for him and Baron von Nucigen's for her. Although he never loves Coralie or Esther as wholeheartedly and absolutely as they love him, Lucien is incapable of hardening his heart sufficiently to exploit them as mercilessly as Collin's plan requires him to do. In the end, it is not his pact with Collin that damns him but the tenderness of his own soul, which cannot bear the awareness that he has repeated his earlier double error, in simultaneously losing a lover and betraying a supposed friend. Love and loyalty are, for Lucien, equally disastrous, because both inhibit the kind of rational pragmatism that is necessary to get by in the *haut monde*.

Balzac always affected to disapprove of that kind of rational pragmatism, even going so far as to represent it as tacitly diabolical, but his choice of a title for the second volume detailing Lucien's checkered career is revealing; the portmanteau text deals not merely with the misery of whores—Esther and Lucien are, of course, both whores—but with their splendors. Esther, a classic example of the literary archetype of the tart with the heart of gold, may seem the more sympathetic of the two to the modern reader, but it was Lucien, in the central section of *Les Illusions perdues*, who embodied and exemplified his author's account of his own lost illusions, even as he took a different path towards a different fate. There is, in consequence, definitely something about Lucien's whoredom—the whoredom of the aspirant dandy—that fascinates and attracts Balzac, almost to the point of obsession. Balzac, unlike Lucien, clung to his literary vocation and eventually made a success of it—but Balzac, unlike Lucien, was not a handsome man, and there remains an obvious element of keen envy in his infinitely painstaking description of Lucien's career. Indeed, that element of envy is so strong as to call into question the superficial judgment that it is Rastignac rather than Lucien who obtains the greater success *as a dandy*.

As Baudelaire pointed out, it is only the dandies in novels who can sustain their status indefinitely, partly because their authors can make them an arbitrary gift of unlimited wealth, and partly because novels can—and, indeed, ought to—conclude at the point of maximal aesthetic satisfaction, while life cannot. Actual nineteenth-century dandies—even those who, like the legendary Robert de Montesquiou, really did have almost-unlimited wealth—were essentially ephemeral, simply because they grew old. Balzac died while the *Comédie humaine*, as he envisaged it, was only half-complete, and never got around to detailing Rastignac's fate, but we know perfectly well what it must have been. He would have begun to show signs of age, and Delphine would have replaced him with a new toy-boy. Even if Victorine had not married in the meantime, she would never have accepted him belatedly as soiled second-hand goods.

Cast aside, he would have plunged abruptly back into poverty, and might well have ended up growing old ignominiously in the same wretched boarding-house from which he started out in *Le Père Goriot*. Lucien, on the other hand, dies at the height of his powers, without even having to compromise his charisma by making the marriage that would have sealed his success.

Lucien's true splendor—the essential splendor of dandyism—is revealed not by any direct description of his costume or his conduct, but by the worshipful attitudes of others. The fourth part of *Splendeurs et misères des courtisanes* is essential to this revelation, partly in detailing the insane and life-threatening grief of Madame de Sérizy—which comfortably exceeds Esther's more dignified resignation in its melodramatic quality—but mainly in describing what becomes of his tempter and mentor, Jacques Collin. Lucien succeeds so well in making himself an object of worship that he gradually seduces his own diabolical seducer, repairing and renewing Jacques Collin's soul to the extent that he is compelled to abandon the cause of prideful opposition and revolt and re-dedicate himself to the dutiful service of the law. (This may seem implausible to some readers, but is perfectly in accordance with French history; the Sûreté—the equivalent of Britain's Scotland Yard-based detective police—was originally made up exclusively of ex-convicts recruited by the Parisian Préfecture de Police as poachers-turned-gamekeepers.)

Jacques Collin was the last in a long series of satanic figures featured in Balzac's works. The author's earlier tales of diabolical pacts had included the most significant of the pseudonymous thrillers he ground out while working as a hack, *Le Centenaire, ou les deux Behringeld* (1822; tr. as *The Centenarian, or the two Behringelds*), the centrepiece of the "philosophical studies" that he integrated into the *Comédie humaine, La peau de chagrin* (1831; tr. as *The Wild Ass's Skin*), and a brief sarcastic sequel to Charles Maturin's Gothic epic *Melmoth the Wanderer* (1820), "Melmoth reconcilié" (1835; tr. as "Melmoth Reconciled"). Balzac had abandoned frank supernaturalism by the time he created Collin, so Collin's diabolical qualities are somewhat muted, but the story-sequence in which he features qualifies nevertheless as a significant precursor of the great tradition of French literary Satanism, which was to be carried forward by Baudelaire and Gustave Flaubert and brought to a peak of attainment by Anatole France.

In all Balzac's previous tales of pacts, including the encounter between Rastignac and Vautrin, the "victims" of the pacts are and remain the focal points of authorial attention, but in Lucien's story the roles are eventually reversed. Like many a fallen angel to feature in subsequent exercises in literary Satanism, Collin falls in love with the victim of his contrived temptation. Collin's homosexuality is as carefully muted as his diabolical status, but no modern reader of *Splendeurs et misères des courtisanes* is likely to be in any doubt about it, and it very nearly becomes explicit in the final part of the sequence. Like Esther and Madame de Sérizy, Collin is ensnared by Lucien's beauty, perfected by the dandyism he has helped Lucien to cultivate, and the young man's death only serves to complete the closure of the trap's deadly jaws.

Living fast, dying young and leaving a beautiful corpse is, for Lucien as for any true dandy, an unmatchable triumph. It enables him to establish a lasting memory—which, although colorfully stained by foolishness and betrayal, is so amenable to exceeding fondness as to occasion an aftermath that no mere dutiful father, beloved husband, military hero or angelic infant son could ever hope to generate. Compared to Lucien, Honoré de Balzac—who had only his literary success and torrents of black coffee to keep him warm—was an abject failure as an object of self-worship, and he obviously knew it.

Charles Baudelaire, who similarly had to settle for literary fame—which was, in his case, largely posthumous—also understood only too well that becoming a great writer was poor compensation, to a man of his perverse stripe, for having failed to become a true dandy, even for a brief moment. It is worth bearing in mind, however, that neither Balzac nor Baudelaire could have become such great writers as they undoubtedly were, had not the envy of dandies been festering away in their souls, lending extravagant fire and furious spite to their fulgurant visions of a world already lost to the ravages of decadence.

# VI.

## THE OSMAZOME OF LITERATURE

In chapter XIV of the Bible of Decadence, Joris-Karl Huysmans' *À rebours*, Jean Des Esseintes claims that of all forms of literature, the prose poem is his favorite. It is, he suggests, the "osmazome" of literature or the "essential oil" of art. (Osmazome was once considered to be the savory principle of flesh, obtainable by selective dissolution in alcohol in much the same way that essential oils are obtained from all manner of vegetable materials.)

Although he has never got around to doing it (action is, after all, a pathetically crude response to the burden of ennui) Des Esseintes has long contemplated the project of condensing a novel to a few sentences by eliminating all the tedious analyses and superfluous descriptions, so that every word that remains would be absolutely unalterable and immovable, each containing multitudinous implications that would need to be read as cleverly as they were written, thus creating the scope for an almost-unique intellectual and imaginative communion between creator and consumer: an aesthetic delight in which only the most discerning individuals could partake.

In an earlier chapter, Des Esseintes has already devoted several pages to an argument hailing Charles Baudelaire as the definitive decadent writer, and he returns to that theme in this passage in chapter XIV, when he picks up an anthology of prose poetry he has compiled for his own use: "a little chapel dedicated to Baudelaire." In addition to Baudelaire's own definitive prose poems he has included therein items by Villiers de l'Isle Adam and Stéphane Mallarmé, and a few choice selections from the work to which French prose poetry owed its origin: Aloysius Bertrand's *Gaspard de la Nuit.*

*Gaspard de la Nuit* was one of Baudelaire's favorite books, and Mallarmé's too; it was the one that inspired both of them to conduct their own experiments in prose poetry. Bertrand does not actually describe his works by means of any equivalent term—even his mentor. Charles-Augustin Sainte-Beuve, confined himself to the descriptive term *ballades en prose*—but the label is nevertheless apt. Had Bertrand done no more than pioneer the form of what came to be known as the prose poem he would have been a vital precursor of Decadent literature; in fact, he did considerably more than that, because, in a few of the items collected in *Gaspard de la Nuit*, and in the notion of Gaspard de la Nuit himself, there are significant seeds of the Decadent world-view.

Louis Bertrand (1807-41) was not among the "poètes maudits" whose valedictory celebration by Paul Verlaine helped Huysmans kick-start the Decadent Movement of the 1880s, but he could have been. Accursed he certainly was, by ill-health and ill-luck alike; he spent the latter years of his life desperately trying to publish *Gaspard de la Nuit*, in order that he might leave behind one solitary book when the tuberculosis from which he had long suffered finally sent him to the grave, but he failed. He had influential advocates, Sainte-Beuve and Victor Hugo among them, but all the deals he made with publishers went awry. Circumstance let him down time and time again, and it was not until he was dead that Sainte-Beuve finally managed to get the book into print, as a memorial to a lost artist, who would surely have done so much more had fate not been so relentlessly intent on tormenting and destroying him.

The sad tale of Bertrand's life and the tragicomedy of his book's long and painful journey to posthumous publication is told in great detail in a new edition of *Gaspard de la Nuit*, adapted into English by the Californian poet Donald Sidney-Fryer, published by Black Coat Press. Sidney-Fryer, the last surviving member of the Californian neo-Romantic school centered on George Sterling, is perfectly qualified to adapt the work of a key member of the French Romantic school, with particular reference to the Decadent elements that had begun to show up in many of the writers who formed the "second generation" of that school as they followed in the giant footprints of Charles Nodier and Victor Hugo, so this edition is a particularly welcome revivification of the classic. Sainte-Beuve—the great pioneer of "psychoanalytic criticism" seeking explanation and enrichment in a writer's personal evolution and travails—would not approve of skipping over the circumstances of an author's life in an article of this sort, but Sidney-Fryer has provided so much context of that kind that I feel free to withdraw to a more distant viewpoint in order to place Bertrand's text within a broader literary panorama.

The book into which Bertrand's literary legacy was assembled by Sainte-Beuve retains the title the author had attached to the shorter text he prepared for publication himself: *Gaspard de la nuit: fantaisies à la manière de Rembrandt et de Callot*. It is signed Aloysius Bertrand because the author always preferred the Medieval version of his given name—much as Georges-Charles Huysmans was later to prefer the Dutch version of his—on the grounds that it made him sound more exotic. The move must have come to seem insufficient, because "Gaspard de la Nuit" is more pseudonym than title; it refers to the hypothetical author of the accumulated *fantaisies*, who is introduced at length in a long prologue.

This prologue—signed Louis Bertrand rather than Aloysius Bertrand—describes a meeting in the author's home town of Dijon with a cunning-faced, mean-seeming and unhealthy character in threadbare clothing, who reminds him of the Wandering Jew. They fall into conversation, and the mysterious stranger reveals that he has been on a quest to "find art" analogous to the Medieval alchemists' quest for the philosopher's stone. After a brief discourse on aesthetics—in which he first asserts that the Devil exists, and holds the key to the quasi-alchemical quest for art; then that the Devil does not exist, and that art is to be found in the heart of God—the stranger hands over the manuscript that comprises the main body of the text. The next day, when the signatory of the introduction goes in search of Gaspard de la Nuit in order to return his "grimoire," no one will give him any information—although everyone seems to recognize the name—until he meets a humpbacked dwarf, who directs him to the house of the parish priest, into which the stranger has allegedly gone, in disguise, to play the tempter, as he once did with Saint Anthony. According to the dwarf, Gaspard de la Nuit is the Devil in person.

If one were to take what the dwarf says at face value, Gaspard de la Nuit would be a key work of literary satanism, preceding Gustave Flaubert's first version of *La Tentation de Saint-Antoine* by some years. Given that the prologue takes every possible precaution to reserve its irresolvable ambiguity, however, one would be unwise to do that. Indeed, there is very little evidence of any kind of diabolical intent in the early pages of the succeeding text, which comprises the *fantaisies* in the manner of Rembrandt. As the book's subtitle indicates, the poet's intention is not to write the kind of ultra-condensed novel that Jean Des Esseintes was later to contemplate, but rather to produce the prose equivalent of a painting: something that could be consumed, as it were, in a single long glance, more a picture in prose than a poem in prose.

Rembrandt van Rijn (1607-1669) was, of course, the great father-figure of realism in art; the leader of the Dutch school that first exploited the technical possibilities of oil painting to produce convincing replications of the texture of actual visual experience. In the prologue, the enigmatic Gaspard supports this kind of artistic project in the speech that begins with his denial that the Devil exists and his insistence that art is to be found in the heart of God. "Monsieur," he says, "we are, ourselves, only the copyists of the Creator." In saying so, he is echoing the thesis of Alexander Baumgarten's pioneering *Aesthetika*, in which the devoted follower of Gottfried Leibniz argued that, since we inhabit the best of all possible worlds, the best art is that which most faithfully imitates the sterling work of the primary Creator. The prologue is, however, followed by a preface—signed Gaspard de la Nuit—which begins unhesitatingly with the assertion that "Art always has two antithetical faces." Rembrandt, the preface proceeds to argue, is only one face of a coin whose other face is Callot.

Jacques Callot (1592-1635) was roughly contemporary with Rembrandt, but he used his brushes in a very different fashion. He was not so much a painter as a sketcher and engraver, not a replicator at all but a caricaturist. Unlike Baumgarten, who thought that all attempts to create "heterocosmically" were necessarily inferior to mimetic reproduction, Callot took an active role in his representations, exaggerating features to which he wanted to draw attention, making the recognizable grotesque. The fashion in which he did so is utterly familiar to us—we see it every day in the work of political cartoonists—but it seemed strange and sinister to many observers of his work in the early seventeenth century.

It is, therefore, the latter phases of Bertrand's strange book—whose original six parts were distributed across a spectrum that moved by degrees from a Rembrandtian pole to a Callotian one—that have something suggestive of the Devil in them, and hence something ready-made to appeal to the imagination of men like Charles Baudelaire and Jean Des Esseintes. I say "original" because the book as it eventually came to exist, posthumously, actually has seven parts, resulting from the fact that Sainte-Beuve added in an extra thirteen items that he thought as worthy of preservation as those Bertrand had selected. Sainte-Beuve's judgment was correct, and there is a sense in which this seventh section extends the spectrum as well as confusing it slightly, because a few of the items contained there are at least as strange and sinister as those Bertrand placed in his own sixth section. (Perhaps Bertrand was being a little too careful to balance his two-faced coin.) In spite of its disruption of the initial scheme, the full text of *Gaspard de la Nuit* is an improvement on Bertrand's own, and serves to demonstrate that, had he lived, he would surely have become a more assiduous follower of Callot than of Rembrandt.

Traces of the Decadent world-view begin to creep into Gaspard de la Nuit's paintings in prose as early as the second section, which introduces "The Fop" and produces ironically skeptical accounts of "Evening Service" and "The Serenade." This corrosive voice becomes gradually more assertive thereafter. The third section—subtitled "Night and her Glamours" is much darker in tone, and its first inclusion, "The Gothic Chamber," introduces a mysterious character named Scarbo. The narrative voice, confined in the eponymous chamber, laments the non-manifestation a whole series of classic hauntings that might have been, because the haunter who actually comes to harass him is "Scarbo, who bites into my neck, and who, to cauterize my bleeding wound, dips into it his finger of red-hot iron".

Scarbo is also featured in the next three items, although he is only named in "Scarbo" and "The Jester." He is a dwarf, as were many of the fools appointed for the amusement of Medieval kings, but when he murmurs into the ears of those who can hear him it is to offer more than a mere reminder of mortality. "Whether you die absolved or damned," he mutters, in the item named for him, "you will have for a shroud a cloth woven by a spider, and I shall enshroud the spider with you!" Subsequently, after promising the hearer a better shroud made from the skin of a serpent, he also promises that "You will hear at your leisure the little children weeping in limbo."

The dwarf disappears thereafter as a physical presence, until he is remanifest in the last of the items that Sainte-Beuve added, but there is a sense in which his voice lingers, ever eager to insert a malicious commentary into the description of scenes that might otherwise be entirely pleasant, reflecting only the benevolence of their divine painter. It is as if, once having been invoked, Scarbo becomes ever-present in spirit, perhaps all the more insistent in his invisibility. His tacit capers haunt the later phases of the third section, providing a kind of insidious rhythm to "Ondine," "The Salamander" and "The Hour of the Sabbath."

The fourth section, "Chronicles," offers bleak views of Medieval life, climaxing in "The Lepers" and "To a Bibliophile," which exude not merely a quintessentially Decadent consciousness of the entropic erosions of time but something of the fascination with "the phosphorescence of putrescence" that was to become one of Baudelaire's proudest hallmarks. The items in the fifth section are displaced in space rather than time, but the same consciousness bursts out in the same manner, most especially in its final item, "The Song of the Mask"—which Jean Lorrain would surely have loved. In the opening lines of this item the narrative voice becomes decisively rather than teasingly Scarboesque: "It is not with a monk's robe and a rosary, but with a jingling tambourine and the garb of a jester, that I myself undertake the adventure of life, this pilgrimage leading to death!" Here, for the first time, there is mention of the curse of ennui, and of the extremes necessary to its evasion.

Although the sixth section begins quietly enough, it swiftly returns to desolation in "On the Rocks of Chèvre-Mort," where we find the poet complaining that "my soul is a wilderness where, on the shore of the abyss, one hand holding onto life and the other holding onto death, I heave a disconsolate sob!" In isolation, this would be mere graveyard self-pity, but it is followed in its turn—after the interlude of "Yet Another Springtime"—with the visionary extravaganza "The Second Man," which begins: "Hell! Hell and paradise! Screams of despair! Screams of joy! Blasphemies of the damned! Harmonies of the chosen!" and goes on—considerably longer than many of its parallel items—to construct a vision of a Creation without humankind, and the apocalyptic destruction thereof.

There is no need for Scarbo here, but it is entirely appropriate that he should reappear in person—in another poem named after him—in the extra seventh section, and that his reappearance should indeed be a return after an apparent absence. "Was I thinking that he had vanished?" the narrative voice asks, after recalling the eponymous monster's jesterish antics as if from a time long past. "The dwarf grew larger between the moon and myself, like the bell-tower of a Gothic cathedral, with a little bell of gold in motion inside its tall pointed hat!" Afterwards, of course, Scarbo vanishes again—but that is his nature, to be always there even when he is not.

In an afterword, Sidney-Fryer suggests that Gaspard and Scarbo are counterparts, Gaspard being a projection of Bertrand's conscious aesthetic quest and Scarbo being an "unself-concious" projection of something darker. Sidney-Fryer suggests that the name is derived from *escarbot*, a dialect term for a dung-beetle (i.e. scarab), and the text of the first "Scarbo" certainly seems to support that contention. But if Gaspard is himself a quasi-diabolical trickster, an ape of God in more than one sense of the phrase, does that not make Scarbo an ape's ape or a fool's fool, threatening an infinite regress of mockery? Here, perhaps, is the element of *Gaspard de la Nuit* that harmonizes most closely with the subsequent flowering of the Decadent world-view: the notion of the world as something not merely spent but excreted, not quite extinct but on the brink of artificial preservation. The Egyptians used to mummify scarabs as well as pharaohs, regarding them as strange symbols of death-as-transfiguration.

Whether one imagines what Bertrand was doing as "painting in prose" or "writing poetry in prose" there can be no doubt that it was calculatedly and quintessentially ambiguous. The hypothetical author, Gaspard de la Nuit is, conceived entirely in terms of *doubles entendres,* flirting—as all ambiguity tends to do when emphasized—with paradoxicality. Gaspard likens his quest to that of the alchemists because their entire business was a matter of contriving exotic combinations and dissolutions, with a view to mastering the art of miraculous transformations. It was a quest that was to be carried forward, consciously and assertively, by other writers, but Arthur Rimbaud's search for an "alchemy of the word" was hardly begun, while Stéphane Mallarmé's grand theory of the supreme Book that would not merely duplicate but embody the continuing creativity of the cosmos was never brought to completion. Perhaps, like the alchemical quest itself, it was doomed to frustration by the implacability of circumstance.

Poetry in prose may seem, on superficial inspection, to be no more than a further step in the evolutionary process that led to "free verse" and "blank verse." That represents the evolutionary process as a matter of progressive abandonment—of rhyme, scansion, linear and stanzal organization—but if it really were no more than that, the end result would actually be prose, and not poetry-in-prose. It would be readable "by eye", with the eye translating directly from symbol to meaning, rather than "by ear," with the eye serving as an intermediary reproducing the sounds of words and the rhythmic qualities of recitation. What Bertrand was trying to do was further to complicate the process of reading rather than simplifying it, as an evolution towards or into prose would have done. He was trying to interpose something akin to the visual contemplation of a painting between symbol and meaning, not instead of the summoning of auditory imagery, but in addition to it. Baudelaire, who was as much an art critic as a poet, and who attempted to sum up his own creative project in a classic essay on "painting modern life," understood what his predecessor was doing—and understood, too, that such redoubled artifice in the process and art of reading might be an invaluable instrument in celebrating the general triumph of artificiality that was a central tenet of decadent consciousness.

The reason why prose-poetry seemed to Jean Des Esseintes to constitute the osmazome of literature and the essential oil of art is that it seeks to demonstrate that a kind of poetic quintessence can not only be retained in the absence of the formal attributes that had earlier seemed to constitute poetry, but might even be strangely transformed by its refinement. The artistry of that quest, as Des Esseintes and Mallarmé both realized and sought to define, is only partly a matter of the auditory dimension of the words and the musicality of their placement; it is also a matter of their quasi-painterly impressionistic and expressionistic suggestiveness.

This is fortunate, from the viewpoint of English readers, for if it were not the case, French prose-poetry would be very difficult indeed to translate. Translation disrupts the auditory dimension of poetry—even if the individual "notes" can be duplicated, the subtle differences in grammar and usage between French and English demand differences in melodic placement—but the suggestiveness that allows prose poetry to reproduce the grotesque-but-recognizable effects of Callot as well as the more carefully-textured effects of Rembrandt does lend itself to translation, at least by a skilful practitioner. Relative to a short story, let alone a novel, prose poetry may seem like sketch-work, but as Rembrandt and Callot both demonstrated—each in his own manner—the best sketch-work can be more flexible and more revealing than work done in the full minutely-nuanced detail of oil-based colors, precisely because it demands a different kind of eyesight on the part of the viewer.

Once its "sketchiness" is appreciated—and there is no pejorative implication in the word in this application—the fact that Decadent writers found prose-poetry an ideal medium becomes more easily explicable. It is for the same reason that they preferred *contes* modeled on folktales to *récits* employing novelistic techniques of narration and depiction in miniature. Decadent prose is, by definition, ornate, but it is also lapidary; it is fascinated by darkness and decay, but in a manner more mordant than morbid, more lackadaisical than lachrymose. The suggestive lines of sketches in words are far more useful to its modes of representation than the minute detailing of quasi-photographic reportage. This is not to say, of course, that it cannot use color, but it uses color in a "sketchy" fashion too, for creative effect rather than reproductive fidelity.

In much the same way that the writers who inspired the Decadent Movement, or who became recruits to it, were naturally drawn to the medium of prose-poetry, so those who invented or have been drawn to prose-poetry have been magnetically drawn to Decadent ways of seeing. This is why Louis Bertrand, like other second-generation Romantics, was drawn in that direction. Had Bertrand survived to write enough material to fill a second book, we can be reasonably certain that the spirit of Scarbo, if not his gnomic presence, would have infused it more mischievously than he infused the work of his counterpart Gaspard de la Nuit. It is a pity that Bertrand did not live long enough to do that, but the work he did accomplish survived him, and spread its seed as liberally as he could have hoped and desired.

# VII.

## THE DEVIL'S DEPARTURE

Gustave Flaubert began writing the first version of *La Tentation de Saint-Antoine* on 24 May 1848, nine days after the Communist uprising in Paris that briefly overturned the French government. Although couched as a drama, it was not intended to be staged, and would easily have defied the ingenuity of anyone who tried to reproduce its phantasmagorical apparatus in the theater. He completed it on 12 September 1849, but he was persuaded by two friends—Maxime Du Camp and Louis Bouilhet—to whom he read it aloud, not to publish it, on the grounds that it was ideologically unsuitable for public consumption.

According to Du Camp's *Souvenirs littéraires* (1881-82)—a painstakingly misleading text that did much to blacken several reputations, most notably Charles Baudelaire's—Bouilhet, speaking on behalf of both men, advised Flaubert to "throw [the manuscript] in the fire and never speak of it again". Flaubert was horrified, protesting that the work was "beautiful", but he bowed to their opinion and set the work aside. It was not the first book he had shelved—he had put away the original version of his first novel, *L'Éducation sentimentale*, on the grounds that it did not adequately reflect his talent and ambition—but that was not the problem with the *Tentation*, which had ambition a-plenty and was by no means ill-written. What horrified Bouilhet and Du Camp was the story's content.

The subject-matter of the *Tentation* had been sanctified by tradition and many a glorious example—Flaubert's direct inspiration was Pieter Brueghel's famous painting, which he had seen in Genoa in

1845—but Flaubert's account of the contest between Satan and the saint was far from orthodox. It is not Anthony but Satan who is the real central character of the first version of the drama, the saint being merely a lens through which the Devil's works can be conveniently and comprehensively viewed. Nor is it at all clear that Anthony's struggle is victorious; the last triumphant speech in the climactic scene is delivered by the Devil, and the last sound echoing about the stage is the laughter of the Adversary—who clearly believes that the dawn that has banished him is a futile interruption that cannot, in the end, deliver Anthony's salvation.

This was not the first time that Flaubert had taken a strong interest in the Devil's works, nor the first time he had allowed Satan to speak at length. The posthumous publication of his earliest writings revealed, in fact, that the *Tentation* was an entirely natural culmination of his literary interests. Satan appears in "Rêve d'enfer" (written 1837), encountered by an alchemist, and has a brief cameo in the rhapsodic "La danse des morts" (written 1838), but gives a much more elaborate account of himself in the phantasmagoric drama "Smarh" (written 1839). Du Camp and Bouilhet probably had not seen these earlier works, but even if they had, they would have judged that the *Tentation* took their argument a step too far, in making too many concessions to the Devil's point of view, thus becoming the first work of explicit literary Satanism that they had ever encountered.

The notion of literary Satanism had allegedly first been broached by William Blake when he commented that John Milton had been "of the devil's party without knowing it"—a comment echoed with considerable approval by Percy Shelley in "A Defence of Poetry" in a passage contending that: "Milton's Devil as a moral being is as far superior to his God, as one who perseveres in some purpose which he has conceived to be excellent in spite of adversity and torture, is to one who in the cold security of undoubted triumph inflicts the most horrible revenge upon his enemy, not from any mistaken notion of inducing him to repent of a perseverance in enmity, but with the alleged design of exasperating him to deserve new torments". Blake, in his "prophetic books", and Shelley, in "Prometheus Unbound", both produced works of literary Satanism, in which rebels against divine authority are elevated as heroes while their opponents are damned as tyrants, but neither had dared to attack the Christian God explicitly or to name his adversary Lucifer, Satan or the Devil.

Flaubert could undoubtedly have protested to his friends—and rightly so—that he was not doing what Blake and Shelley had attempted to do. Indeed, his first and foremost conviction was that writers should not make moral judgments at all—that they should present the incidents of their story as objectively as possible, leaving readers to make up their own minds as to what lessons might be drawn therefrom. Du Camp and Bouilhet could, however, have replied that there was a sense in which that was even worse: that a refusal to take sides between God and Satan, in favor of compiling an objective record of the tactics of temptation and the argumentative resources that might be marshaled in the contest for Anthony's soul, was a heresy more dangerous to faith than any mere delight in rebellion or sin—and they, too, would have been right. To suspend judgment on the contest between virtue and sin is a fundamental betrayal of faith; to refuse to take it for granted that good is superior to evil is more profoundly subversive than a decision to choose evil for self-indulgent reasons.

Does this mean that Du Camp and Boulihet were right, and that Flaubert should have burned his book? Had he taken the problem to his confessor, it is likely that he would have received the same advice, but he did not, and wisely so. Flaubert was right, and faith was wrong; artists, unlike churchmen, should not take anything for granted, and should be prepared to suspend even those judgments that seem most obvious to others. It is precisely because what Flaubert had attempted to do in the *Tentation* was so profoundly unsettling that it was worth doing, and needed doing. That is why he did not burn the manuscript, but merely put it away until the time was ripe, turning his attention instead to a much more prosaic tale of temptation: *Madame Bovary*.

Charles Baudelaire, who had not yet become the great pioneer of Decadent style, had allegedly greeted the 1848 rebellion in his own unique style. According to Maxime Du Camp, he had put on a workman's blouse and set himself to race from barricade to barricade, attempting to rally a mob to murder his stepfather, General Aupick. Alas, no mob would oblige him—again according to the dubious testimony of Du Camp—thus, presumably, assisting in the amplification of Baudelaire's notion of himself as a man victimized by an evil fate that wore the hypocritical mask of virtue. Among the early poems Baudelaire had penned before 1848—although it was not published until it appeared in *Les Fleurs du mal* in 1857, and Flaubert could not have known of its existence when he penned the *Tentation*—was a work of uncompromisingly explicit literary Satanism, "Les Litanies de Satan".

Unlike Flaubert, Baudelaire did not believe that he had any duty to maintain the moral neutrality of his art—indeed, he gave far more attention to comment than mere description, and all his reportage was steeped in black sarcasm—so he had no qualms about siding with Satan against God. On the other hand, he insisted that he was "an incorrigible Catholic", who never lapsed from the faith, so his preference for Satan was apparently predicated on an underlying assumption of the necessity of God. Even so, there is much in Baudelaire's work that is strongly in sympathy with Flaubert's; sarcasm of the kind that Baudelaire favored is, in essence, built on a cynical withdrawal from all commonplace judgment, and it aspires to a kind of objectivity that is only possible in artistry.

Coincidentally, *Madame Bovary* and *Les Fleurs du mal* were published in the same year, and both of them were prosecuted for offending public decency: a charge that both authors denied vehemently. The cuts demanded by the courts with respect to both books were soon restored in subsequent editions ("Les Litanies de Satan" was not one of the poems whose removal from *Les Fleurs du mal* was demanded, the court being more concerned with erotic matters) but the temporary excisions made their mark. The two writers, who had not previously been acquainted, were introduced to one another's work—after Flaubert's condemnation but before Baudelaire's—by Théophile Gautier, although they could not meet in the flesh at that time because Flaubert was at Croisset and did not plan to return to Paris until the winter.

After reading *Les Fleurs du mal*, Flaubert wrote to Baudelaire complimenting him on the "refinements" of his language, but added some further compliments of a more distinctive kind: "You write of the flesh without loving it, in a melancholy, detached way that I find sympathetic. You are as unyielding as marble and as penetrating as an English fog." When Flaubert heard, a month later, that *Les Fleurs du mal* had suffered the same fate as *Madame Bovary*, he wrote to say that he was "deeply indignant"; Baudelaire, for his part, set to work on a defensive review of *Madame Bovary*—a review in which Flaubert believed that the book "is understood and felt to its very depths". Baudelaire was particularly impressed by the way in which Flaubert had divested himself of his own world-view in order to assume that of his character: an act of imaginative re-identification that had never been attempted before, and represented, in his view, a renaissance of the novel as an art-form (he had previously opined that the novel had died with Balzac).

There is a certain irony in the fact that the two books attacked by the French courts in 1857 became the foundation-stones of two divergent literary traditions. While *Les Fleurs du mal* became the great exemplar of Decadent style and the ultimate inspiration of the Symbolist Movement, *Madame Bovary* became the paradigm example of the naturalistic novel, a key example of a new kind of narrative realism. By the end of the century, they were the shibboleths of two rival schools of literary endeavor, repositioned as poles apart, but they began their careers united, in the public mind and in the minds of their creators, as two manifestations of a single kind of literary eyesight, possessed of a new clarity, a new penetration and—above all else—an adamantine determination to see things as they were, and not through the lens of any kind of pretence intended to misrepresent them.

Flaubert had already returned his attention to the *Tentation* when the *Madame Bovary* scandal erupted, and had produced a second draft—but the rewritten version was reluctantly set aside, just as the first had been; he went on to write the historical novel *Salammbô* (1862) instead. By the time that novel was published, the reputation of *Madame Bovary* was secure and a second edition of *Les Fleurs du mal* had restored the poems removed in 1857, but Baudelaire's health was failing under the assaults of syphilis—a disease that Flaubert had also contracted, but which spared him its worst effects for some time to come. Having published *Salammbô*, Flaubert returned yet again to the manuscripts on his shelf, but not to the *Tentation*; he set out to produce a very different and conscientiously updated version of *L'Éducation sentimentale* for publication in 1869. He was deeply disappointed by its critical reception, but that probably reinforced his determination to rescue the *Tentation* from obscurity. Although he was afflicted in the early 1870s by a chain of personal catastrophes—including the death of his mother, who had long supported him in his literary endeavors, in 1872—he eventually set out to produced a third and final version of the text, which he published in 1874.

By that time, of course, Flaubert was in a frame of mind quite different from the one that had driven him to produce the first version, partly because his personal circumstances had changed so drastically, but partly because the condition of France was so very different. The democratic government set up after the 1848 revolution had metamorphosed into the Second Empire as a result of Louis Napoléon's *coup d'état*, and the Empire had come crashing down under the merciless assault of Bismarck's guns at the battle of Sedan in September 1870; during the subsequent siege of Paris the Commune had seized power in March 1871, only to be bloodily deposed two months later. Perhaps, given all this, it is not surprising that the ultimate text of the *Tentation* is even more distanced and objective in its tone, as well more efficient in its organization, than the first. It is, admittedly, equipped with a markedly different and considerably more diplomatic ending—Saint Anthony, who has been a more active character throughout, counters Satan's wiles so cleverly that he ends the text fearless and blissful, ready to greet the face of Jesus beaming out from the newly-risen sun—but if it is read attentively enough, it is no less subversive than its predecessor.

It still seems to many readers that it is the earlier version of the *Tentation* that is more in tune with the Decadent world-view—which is, of course, essentially adversarial and therefore committed to the kind of literary Satanism featured in Baudelaire's "Litanies"—but the later one is by no means entirely discordant with it, because the manner of Satan's apparent defeat is by no means a triumph of piety, let alone of faith; it is, instead, a triumph of objectivity.

By the time the drama of the *Tentation* begins, Anthony's material resources have been reduced to a bare minimum; his *modus vivendi* has been stripped of all but the most basic necessities. His elevated platform reflects, metaphorically, the state of his soul, scoured by circumstance as by a desert wind, surrounded by immovable boulders; the only living thing in his vicinity is a single palm tree and the only significant artifact a wooden cross. In both versions of the text, the visions that the Devil sends to afflict him displace him in time, by carrying him "back" to places he knew as a younger man, in the private world of his imagination, by allowing him access to fantastic entities, and in space, showing him the true magnitude of the universe and the smallness of the human world within it. The balance between these three directions of displacement is, however, markedly different and more finely calculated in the final version.

The places to which Anthony is taken include Alexandria, the former capital of Egypt. He is transported to the Panium—an artificial mound in the city center overlooking Lake Mareotis—where he sees the monks of the Thebaïd invade the city to kill the Arian heretics. He joins the slaughter, subsequently enjoying the hospitality of the Emperor Constantine, but the temptation of power is insufficient to claim his soul, so he is removed instead to a vast Basilica in which the Christian faithful are gathered, where Manes—the author of the Manichaean heresy—is preaching from a throne of gold. Manes is succeeded by other heretics, who eventually succeed in rousing the entire crowd to murderous violence, but Anthony resists. Outside the Basilica he meets more exotic heretics and representatives of many other religious traditions, but still he cannot be dislodged from his own faith. Ultimately, the Devil carries Anthony away from the Earth. They pass by the moon—a luminous sphere resembling a ball of ice—into the infinite realm of the stars.

Elevation to this lofty standpoint within an immensity of darkness is supposed to prove to Anthony the utter irrelevance of the Earth, and hence of humankind, within the universe. It comes close to achieving that end—but the second version offers a much more elaborate account of this part of the narrative than the first, and adds another aspect to the visionary odyssey which is only briefly trailed in the original, as a speech made by "Science". When Anthony is returned to his hovel his vision becomes truly phantasmagoric, as he is assailed by the phantoms of his own imagination, but these take different forms in the two versions. In the earlier one, pagan deities and personalizations of the seven deadly sins raise a terrible clamor, but in the later one, brief appearances by Death and Lust are soon displaced by a parade of bizarre monsters.

It may seem, at first glance, that Satan comes off far worse in the second version than the first. He is not even on stage during the final act, having quit the scene at the end of the sixth part—"The Mystery of Space"—after challenging Anthony not merely with a vision of the universe but with the philosophical possibility that the phenomenal world might be an "illusion of [his] intellect". The final parade of monsters is left without a diabolical commentary—or, rather, Anthony is left alone with the reader to draw his own conclusions. In their own fashion, the apparitions that are displayed to Anthony in the last section of the published version are even more horrifying than the cacophonous voices that clamored for his attention in the first, but Anthony has the resources to deal with them. The crucial irony underlying the final act is that those resources were gifted to him not by any faith in God or hope of salvation, but by the Devil himself, as a result of their voyage into the remoter realms of the cosmos.

What makes the crucial difference between the two versions of Anthony's temptation, in Flaubert's final analysis, is that the saint is able to respond to the monsters that mock him in his final vision—not merely "The Chimera and the Sphinx" for whom the final part is titled but the headless blemmyes, the half-vegetable sciapodes, the dog-headed cynocephali, the many-antlered sadhuzag, the mantichor, the catoblepas, the griffin and dozens more—not with terror but with wonder, and at least the beginnings of understanding. Whereas the speech of Science, in the first version, was immediately followed and seemingly subverted by the oration of Pride, Anthony is able in the final version to make his observations coolly, unafflicted by any such tumult. He is able to convert the vision in his mind's eye into a holistic panorama of life, in which animals become indistinguishable from plants and plants from minerals: an ecological free-for-all in which the fervor of creation is everywhere manifest. The fecundity of Earthly life needs no commentary; it speaks for itself—and what it says allows Anthony to attain an ecstasy whose symbolism by the final image of Christ's face is blatantly hypocritical.

"Oh bliss! bliss! I have seen the birth of life," Anthony says, in his final speech. "I have seen the origin of motion. The blood beats so powerfully in my veins that it seems about to burst through. I feel the urge to fly, to swim, to bark, to bellow, to howl. I would that I had wings, a turtle's shell, a rind; that I were able to blow out vapor, possess a trunk, coil my body; to spread myself out, encompassing every place and every thing, emanating all odors; to flow like water, vibrate like sound, radiate like light; to be outlined in every form, penetrate every atom, descend into the very depths of matter—to be matter!"

The Devil has already departed in advance of this meditation, not because he has been defeated but because he has become irrelevant. He has not bested Anthony, because Anthony has seen that there is, in fact, no contest. The saint no longer needs to be persuaded one way or the other, nor can he be; science is no longer a voice contending with all the rest but an attitude of mind that quiets all such voices with a perception that is not merely clear but blissful. Although the face of Jesus might have replaced the Devil's mocking laughter as a final theatrical gesture, it is no more relevant to the conclusion of the argument than its predecessor. Anthony has transcended the very possibility of temptation, from either side—and that is a more extreme form of literary Satanism than any mere Devil could ever contrive.

Although the basic story-line of *Madame Bovary* was borrowed from provincial newspaper reports of a real case, Flaubert often replied, when asked whether he had a model in mind for Emma Bovary, that she was himself. What he meant was that his own imagination had been excited by Romantic notions of much the same kind as those that led his foolish heroine astray; like her he had become desperate for a means of escaping from the appalling ennui of provincial life. He found his own escape not so much in his various expeditions as in the work of literary composition in which he immersed himself profoundly—more profoundly, his letters suggest, than any writer had previously contrived to do.

Like Emma Bovary, Anthony was Flaubert; as Baudelaire observed, Flaubert's triumph as an artist was the ability to become his characters—to efface his own world-view in favor of theirs, to function as a "method actor" in print. In the 1848 version of the *Tentation*, the temptations offered by the Devil were all the more attractive for their purely imaginary character, and within the theater of the imagination there was no way that ordinary virtue could prevail against them. In that version, although Anthony resists damnation, the Devil is indeed the effective winner of their contest and we leave Anthony wailing "Pity! Pity!" In 1848, Flaubert's assertion that a writer must hold to a position of neutrality was not yet personally sustainable; there were too many voices and too many visions clamoring for his attention. By the time he prepared the 1874 version of the *Tentation* for publication, however, Flaubert was in his fifties, and his own triumph over the temptations of Romanticism was complete—sufficiently so, at any rate, for the Devil to have become a figure of intellectual rather than passionate interest, whose tactics and devices could be described and analyzed in an authentically clinical fashion. The author had achieved his Age of Reason, and his Age of Enlightenment; he really was capable of standing aside from all opinion and all faith, in order to see life as it is. In his own person, he was victim to many misfortunes, recent and ongoing; his homeland was in a parlous state, having suffered the most humiliating defeat in its history—but when he assumed the situation of Saint Anthony, whose torments were temptations, for the third time in his life, he would not yield. This time, he would not ask for pity; this time, he held out for bliss—and found it where he could.

In all its versions, the *Tentation* is an allegory of self-discovery, in which the human intellect and imagination are battered and besieged by all the doubts that intellect and imagination can raise. Flaubert differs sharply from other writers of Faustian fantasies, however, in taking it for granted that the temptations of wealth and sex—the former represented by a cup and coins, the latter by the

Queen of Sheba and Ennoïa (the companion of Simon Magus)—are by no means the most powerful levers that can be applied against virtue. When other writers add further lures to these (and few have seen the need) they usually do so by adding even-more-extreme sensations, but Flaubert is more interested in purely intellectual temptations: paganism and heresy. The bribery implicit in Simon's magic is easy enough for Anthony to resist, but the mockery of Apollonius of Tyana is much harder. Who could blame the Devil, in the final version, for thinking that, if he could only take one more step in that direction, even this stern man's resolve might break? Who could blame Satan for thinking that a vision of the actual cosmos—the ultimate heresy, in the eyes of the churchmen who persecuted Galileo—might do the trick? But who, reading the text as Flaubert must have written it, identifying as fully with Anthony as possible, can refuse to understand why the trick backfired?

Even in the earlier version, the Devil's victory does not consist of carrying Anthony off to Hell in the vulgar fashion of some Gothic shocker, but merely in granting him the intellectual legacy of his discoveries—thus condemning him to live with the sound of diabolical laughter forever resounding in his ears. In the final analysis, Anthony is immunized against that laughter, and all its Hellish implications, by virtue of having perceived a further truth, and having come into the true legacy of his discovery. Between 1848 and 1874 Flaubert had found his own intellectual and artistic security, and that achievement is resoundingly echoed in the ultimate conclusion of the work that took him half a lifetime to complete.

Having said all that, though, it must also be said that Maxime Du Camp and Louis Bouilhet were entirely wrong to tell Flaubert that his work was unpublishable, and that it ought to be burned. Even in the first version—whose virtue can be measured via René Francis's translation of the 1856 manuscript, published in English as *The First Temptation of Saint Anthony* by the Bodley Head in 1924, which include the passages dropped from the 1848-49 text as a series of appendices—the drama is an artistic triumph; it is, as Flaubert complained to his friends, quite beautiful. The fact that we now have all the texts to compare with one another, in fact, adds considerably to our appreciation of the work. Had we not seen what might have become of Anthony, if he had not matured so completely and fruitfully, we could not judge the extent of his mastery half as well. Indeed, if we did not know that the alternative ending to the one that has become definitive was the inescapability of Satan's laughter, we might fall into the trap of taking the apparition of Jesus at the end of the 1874 text far more seriously than is necessary or justified—as many of its unwary contemporary readers presumably did.

# VIII.

## TWIN SOULS IN TORMENT

Charles Baudelaire issued the first of his many translations of Edgar Poe in 1848. In February of that year he had briefly taken his place on the barricades, after seeing a national guardsman impale one of the Parisian revolutionaries with a bayonet, but his involvement in the conflict did not last much beyond June, when disillusion had set in. His translation of Poe's "Mesmeric Revelation" appeared in the 15 July issue of *La Liberté de Penser*.

Baudelaire had first encountered Poe's fiction in the previous year, in a short series of translations by Isabelle Meunier that had appeared in *La Démocratie pacifique*. His interest must have been aroused immediately, but it was not until he began to read Poe's poetry and criticism in 1852 that he began to feel the strong sense of kinship that inspired more extensive involvement. By that time, Poe had been dead for four years, and Baudelaire had discovered certain circumstances of the author's biography reminiscent of his own situation. Like Baudelaire, Poe had lost his father in early childhood, and had been saddled with an unsympathetic stepfather, formulating his art and lifestyle in the face of manifest disapproval and calculated obstruction. Like Baudelaire, Poe had accepted poverty as the price of his literary commitment, fighting a long losing battle against the desire to keep up appearances socially and sartorially, and a parallel battle against the calumnies of contemporary writers resentful of his iconoclastic tendencies.

Baudelaire published a eulogistic account of Poe's life and works in the March and April 1952 issues of the *Revue de Paris*—

his first appearance in that prestigious periodical—and his translation of "Berenice" appeared in the 17 April issue of *L'Illustration*. His version of "The Pit and the Pendulum" was in the *Revue de Paris* in October, and the pace of his similar endeavors accelerated steadily thereafter; four translated stories appeared in 1853, ten in 1854, and eighteen more in the first three months of 1855.

Baudelaire's determination to publish a definite collection of his poetry never waned in the meantime, but after he published a batch of eleven poems in April 1851 only three more reached print until he published a new batch of eighteen—using the title *Les Fleurs du mal* for the first time—in June 1855. When the book version of *Les Fleurs du mal* was published in June 1857 it came hot on the heels of a translation of *The Narrative of A. Gordon Pym*, which had completed its serialization in *Le Moniteur universel* in April, and Baudelaire's second collection of Poe's tales, *Nouvelles histoires extraordinaires*, issued by Michel Lévy in March (Lévy published the *Pym* translation in volume form the following year).

Many of the poems featured in *Les Fleurs du mal* had been written much earlier; Baudelaire had already determined the subject-matter and manner of his own work before encountering Poe; such influence as Poe had on the formulation of Baudelaire's work was limited, and not fully expressed until Baudelaire began to compile and collate the material for his intended collection of prose poems, *Spleen de Paris*. For an interval of two-and-a-half years in the long run-up to the publication of his own masterpiece, however, Baudelaire gave himself over almost entirely to the translation of works by his American *alter ego*, binding himself to the same world-view and the same philosophy of procedure.

It is possible that Baudelaire was mistaken about Poe's actual literary method. If Poe's essay on "The Philosophy of Composition" is a satirical hoax offering a sarcastic counterpoint to Samuel Taylor Coleridge's account of the inspirational composition of "Kubla Khan", Baudelaire probably took it too seriously—but that is a matter of scant importance, given that the real kinship between the two was more deeply ingrained; the important thing about "decadent style" is not the mechanics of its production but the psychological roots of its motivation.

Baudelaire's account of Poe's ideas in the 1852 essay reads rather oddly, but that had less to do with any misconceptions Baudelaire may have had about Poe's philosophy of literature than his desire to co-opt Poe's support for his own dissent from Théophile Gautier's philosophy of "*l'art pour l'art*"—whose central dictum, as restated in the preface to *Mademoiselle de Maupin*, was ultimately to be paraphrased by Oscar Wilde as "all art is quite useless". Baudelaire did not believe that, and he was enthusiastic to cast Poe as a fellow-believer in the utility of art. (There was probably an element of retaliation in Gautier's preface to the posthumous third edition of *Les Fleurs du mal*; Gautier's analysis of Baudelaire's decadent style can be read, if one is so minded, as an attempt to reclaim the poet for the school of "*l'art pour l'art*"—a move that many later writers, including Wilde, deemed successful.)

What Baudelaire meant by the "utility" of art was not the vulgar utility of mundane didacticism, but something more refined. What he thought "useful" in Poe was the particular kind of mysticism that Poe embraced in the "Mesmeric Revelation" and expanded to its fullest expression in his long essay *Eureka*. Baudelaire gave a fuller account of this alleged commitment to utility in his introduction to his translation of "Berenice", where he offered "rabid inquisitiveness" as a synonymous phrase and went on to compliment Poe's interest in "mental disorders, speculative sciences, and prospects for...the afterlife".

Baudelaire's subsequent translations were done with this attitude of mind established as a base. The most crucial exemplars of Poe's own development of the idea of decadence and the decadent style were not among Baudelaire's earliest translations; his version of "The Fall of the House of Usher" appeared in *Le Pays* in February 1855, immediately followed in the same publication by his versions of "The Masque of the Red Death" and "The Murders in the Rue Morgue"—although he must have read them some time before. The groundwork for his translation of these paradigm examples of Poesque decadence had, however, been well-laid; his version of "The Imp of the Perverse" had appeared in *Le Pays* the previous September, three days after "The Cask of Amontillado" and three days before "Metzengerstein". If we are to consider Poe's influence on Baudelaire's notion of decadent thematics and stylistics, as well as his own development of the decadent world-view, we need to bear in mind the fact that Baudelaire did not produce his versions in the same order that Poe produced his, and that the lens of the "Mesmeric Revelation" must have influenced the way he saw them in a way that the story in question could not possibly have influenced Poe's prior vision.

Several key ideas relating to the decadent world-view can be found in "Metzengerstein", which was Poe's first published short story, originally appearing in 1832. It tells of two ancient houses locked in a centuries-old feud, and of how the "Palace Metzengerstein" becomes the scene of a three-day orgy of "shameful debaucheries" and "unheard-of atrocities" when young baron Frederick comes into his inheritance, climaxing in the burning of his rival's stables. As the story unfolds, the baron becomes obsessed with a mysterious horse that first appeared on the night of the fire, which carries him away when his own home is consumed in its turn.

Baudelaire might have encountered similar imagery for the first time in "Berenice", first published in 1835, in which Poe extrapolated the decadent motifs of "Metzengerstein" considerably. The protagonist of "Berenice" relates that he was raised in "time-honored...gloomy, grey, hereditary halls" less grandiose but no less portentous than Palace Metzengerstein, and it soon becomes obvious that he is similarly infected—along with his eponymous cousin—with hereditary maladies that have grown increasingly toxic with the passing of the generations. It is in "Berenice", too, that Poe's highly mannered style makes important progress; Baudelaire must have been particularly impressed by the narrative's apparent inspiration by a quotation from Tertullian's *De Carne Christi*—one of the esoteric classics of the Latin Decadence, written in the 3rd century A.D.—and presumably enjoyed his languid intercourse with the narrative's decorative prose.

Baudelaire might not have been so impressed, when he eventually got around to translating "The Fall of the House of Usher" (1839), to discover its apparent inspiration in a line from a song by his own older contemporary Pierre-Jean de Béranger, on whose work he had always poured scorn. He could not, however, have taken exception to the manner in which Poe developed the borrowed image of a heart strung like a lute, resonant to the slightest touch. Nor can he have been disappointed by the flagrant eccentricity of the extensive reading-list offered within the story. The latter leads off with a slightly-confused citation of Jean-Baptiste Gresset's mock epic *Ver-vert*—about a parrot that scandalizes a convent with bad language—and goes on to juxtapose Niccolo Machiavelli with Emmanuel Swedenborg, Ludwig Holberg's account of Nils Klim's subterranean adventures with Robert Fludd's textbook of cheiromancy, and a Romantic fantasy by Ludwig Tieck with Tomasso Campanella's Utopian *City of the Sun*. It drops in the stubbornly obscure and probably fictitious "Jean D'Indaginé and...Dela Chambre" *en passant*, before concluding with a guide to inquisitorial practice compiled by the Dominican friar Eymeric de Gironne and the more imaginative components of Pomponius Mela's pioneering textbook of geography.

It is in this story that the equivalence of an edifice about to fall into ruins and its ultimate heir—whose "*morale*" explicitly reflects his environment's "*physique*"—is taken to an explicit extreme. The account of the unfolding of that equivalence is not offered by the sufferer, in such a manner that it might pass for subjective delusion; the narrator is a relatively objective witness, although he is also a catalyst. It is, in fact, the narrator's reading aloud from an imaginary chivalric romance, Sir Launcelot Canning's "The Mad Trist", whose echoes in the fabric of the mansion provoke its disintegration and awaken Madeline Usher from her death-sleep. Much has been made by critics of the role played in Roderick Usher's ruination by his presumed incestuous desire for Madeline—continuing a long family tradition, if the branchlessness of the Usher line is anything to go by—but Baudelaire would surely have noted that the disaster is actually precipitated, and precisely formulated, by a reading whose contents celebrate the ideals incarnate in the French nation's Charlemagnian creation-myth—feudal ideals whose long and conclusive decay had reached an apparent terminus in the post-Napoleonic nineteenth century.

It was to this long-lost feudal past that Poe was to return in his most extravagant exemplar of decadent style, "The Masque of the

Red Death" (1842), which describes the annihilation of a corrupt relic of the baronial ideal. Prince Prospero, unlike Roderick Usher and his patient lector, is no devotee of reading, and his heart is quite insensitive to any emotional vibration. His favored distraction is a masquerade of conspicuous splendor, and the story's only literary reference is a brief aside that attempts to convey something of the grotesque spirit of its costumery by comparing the display to Victor Hugo's classic of Romantic theatricality *Hernani*—at whose premi̇ère, as both Poe and Baudelaire would have been conscious, Théophile Gautier had appeared in a calculatedly-scandalous red waistcoat.

In between "The Fall of the House of Usher" and "The Masque of the Red Death" Poe published "The Murders in the Rue Morgue" (1841), set in contemporary Paris and featuring a protagonist very different from the neurotic hypochondriacs and delusional obsessives of his earlier decadent fantasies. Auguste Dupin is now celebrated as the first great literary detective, whose deductive approach to the solution of a mysterious double murder is based on a method of inquiry described in the "memoirs" of François-Eugène Vidoq (1775-1857), the first volume of which—originally issued in 1828—had recently been translated into English.

Before looking at "The Murders in the Rue Morgue" in more detail, it is worth digressing to consider the peculiar career of M. Vidocq, whose legend would have been very familiar to Baudelaire when he first encountered Poe. Vidocq was essentially a writer of sensational fiction, but he disguised his work as autobiography, following precedents set by the most popular French writer of the 1820s, Étienne-Léon Lamothe-Langon.

Lamothe-Langon had begun his career as a sensation-monger by improvising the memoirs that Louis XV's most notorious mistress, the Comtesse du Barry, had never troubled to write, sparing no effort in making them more colorful than the lady in question would have countenanced. He followed up his first triumph with other exercises in a similar vein, but there were few actual individuals with as much ready-made charisma as the Comtesse du Barry; although the author took care to embellish his succeeding volumes with some memorable inventions, he soon attempted to move into fresher fields.

In developing more nearly-contemporary settings Lamothe-Langon had to be careful of offending the living, but he found abundant scope for deceptive circumspection in recording the reminiscences of *L'Espion de Police* [The Police Spy] in 1826, taking advantage of the cloak of secrecy that shrouded all police operations in those days. It was undoubtedly this book that prompted Vidocq to write his own "memoirs", which relate how he set off for America with 2,000 francs stolen from his father but was robbed and reduced to destitution, after which he kept company with vagabonds, entered the service of a famous acrobat, enlisted in the army, deserted, and then became a thief in Paris, enjoying such a successful career that when he offered his expertise to the police in 1809 the Prefecture was delighted by the prospect of obtaining the services of such an expert poacher-turned-gamekeeper. Vidocq claimed that, after initially being put in charge of four men he eventually progressed to the command of a squad of twenty-four, which constituted the original Sûreté Publique, before resigning in 1827 and ceding his place to his loyal lieutenant, Coco-Lacour.

Although Vidocq's memoirs were successful by the standards of the day, popular fiction had not yet become the money-spinner that it was destined to be, once Alexandre Dumas and Eugène Sue had revealed the potential of the *roman feuilleton*. According to a second account of his adventures that he published in 1844, revealingly entitled *Vrais mystères de Paris* (Sue's classic *Mystères de Paris* had finished its epoch-making serialization in October 1843) Vidocq allegedly offered to serve his country again in the wake of the July revolution of 1830, this time in Louis-Philippe's political police. His second set of "memoirs" reveals that he used the privileges of his new position to arrange an unprecedentedly daring series of crimes, supposedly in order to make a case for returning to his old job, before being sacked by the Prefect when his responsibility was divined.

After the revolution of 1848, according to Pierre Larousse's famous encyclopedia (published during in the 1870s), Vidocq offered his services yet again to the new government, but the offer was rejected. Whoever wrote the Larousse entry frankly opined that Vidocq's memoirs contained *"beaucoup de faits de pure invention"*, and the fact that their two components manifestly tried to cash in on recent successes by Lamothe-Langon and Sue strongly implies that they ought to be reckoned as works of fiction, but their readers were not so sure. Historians, faced with a dearth of potentially-contradictory evidence; have not been so sure either; to this day, Vidocq is widely credited with having invented the Sûreté and—more importantly, in the context of "The Murders in the Rue Morgue"—having pioneered its methods of detection, by methodically analyzing the "clues" unthinkingly left behind by the perpetrators of crimes.

The deductive method of detection was already in the process of replacing the inquisitorial method that had been in place for centuries, because it was more in keeping with the modern idea of "proof"—borrowed from the new science of the Age of Reason—than older ideas based in such institutions as trial by ordeal. The French police had begun to conduct enquiries of his kind before the revolution of 1789—as evidenced by the abundant documentation of such cases as the infamous "affair of the necklace", in which Cardinal de Rohan had been conned out of a large sum of money allegedly to be used to commission a diamond necklace for Marie Antoinette—but Vidocq's assumption that they could and would be further refined in future was undeniably astute. His demonstration that fiction was a far more appropriate medium than reality ever could be for such methods to reach their finest pitch of achievement was equally astute, as Poe realized as soon as he had read the memoirs (Vidocq is cited by name in "The Murders in the Rue Morgue"). Poe set out to design a series of fictitious "cases" that would put the deductive method to a more rigorous proof than any trial by ordeal that the hypothetical Sir Launcelot Canning could ever have devised for his valiant knight, Sir Ethelred.

"The Murders in the Rue Morgue" begins with a quotation from Sir Thomas Browne relating to famously insoluble mysteries ("what song the Syrens sang, or what name Achilles assumed when he hid himself among women") and launches into a long prefatory essay on the analytical "faculty of re-solution", as applied to enigmas and to games of chess and whist—an argumentative idyll that contrasts strongly with Poe's denunciation of the limitations of induction and deduction in the introduction to *Eureka*. Dupin is then introduced, as a "young gentleman" of an illustrious family now fallen on hard times, who hoards his meager resources in order to assure his supply of his most cherished luxury: books. The narrator encounters him in a library, and is admitted into his society in order to shore up his exceedingly limited means.

"As my worldly circumstances were somewhat less embarrassed than his own," the narrator records, "I was permitted to be at the expense of renting, and furnishing in a style which suited the rather fantastic gloom of our common temper, a time-eaten and grotesque mansion, long deserted through superstitions into which we did not enquire, and tottering to its fall....

"Had the routine of our life at this place been known to the world, we should have been regarded as madmen.... Our seclusion was perfect.... We existed within ourselves alone.

"It was a freak of fancy in my friend...to be enamored of the night for her own sake; and into this *bizarrerie*, as into all his others, I quietly fell, giving myself up to his wild whims with perfect *abandon*. The sable divinity could not herself dwell with us always; but we could counterfeit her presence. At the first dawn of the morning we closed all the massy shutters of our old building and lighted a couple of tapers which, strongly perfumed, threw out only the ghastliest and feeblest of rays. By the aid of these we then busied our souls in dreams—reading, writing, or conversing—until warned by the clock of the advent of the true Darkness."

Following this sketch of an ideal Gothic lifestyle—clearly prompted by the Imp of the Perverse that Poe knew and understood so well—the narrator offers further comments on Dupin's analytical tendencies and their manifestation as an alternative state of consciousness. This puts him in mind of "the old philosophy of the Bi-Part soul", Dupin's being one in which "the creative and the resolvent" exist in uneasy balance. This leads in turn into an anecdote in which Dupin "reads" the narrator's train of thought by following a sequence of his momentary sensory experiences and guessing the connected series of ideas thus prompted, setting the stage for their discovery of a newspaper report of the mysterious double murder in the Rue Morgue.

The remainder of the story is no real significance with respect to the decadent world-view. After visiting the scene of the crime—during which the narrator notices nothing in particular—the two return home, where Dupin embarks on a long explanation of what *he* has noticed, and what he has concluded on the basis of his observations. He has already summoned the custodian of the crime's perpetrator to the house, and there follows a confrontation in which all is explained and prepared for settlement. The story concludes by mocking the unfortunate Prefect of Police—who has, of course, reached an entirely mistaken conclusion as to the guilty party—with a quotation from Jean-Jacques Rousseau's *La nouvelle Héloîse*, which accuses him of "denying that which is and explaining that which is not".

Seen, with the aid of hindsight, as the foundation-stone of the detective genre, "The Murders in the Rue Morgue" might seem a straightforward hymn of praise to rigorous deduction, in which a pre-Holmesian elimination of the impossible leads inexorably to a conclusion which, however unlikely, must be true. From this point of view, however, the characterization of Dupin's lifestyle and bipartite soul seem quite superfluous, as well as decidedly odd. Baudelaire, reading the story in the early 1850s, had no such hindsight to guide him, but he did know that, three years after publishing "The Murders in the Rue Morgue", Poe had published the "Mesmeric Revelation", extolling an intuitive, if not frankly supernatural, means of cutting through the fog of appearances to reach the truth.

To Baudelaire, therefore, Dupin's peculiar attitude of mind and mental make-up must have seemed crucial to his achievement in "re-solving" the crime—all the more so given the remarkable insight evidenced in his prior analysis of the narrator's train of thought, which has far more inspired guesswork in it than authentic observation or deductive analysis. This must have made it far easier for Baudelaire—as it undoubtedly had for Poe—to see himself symbolically represented in the character of Auguste Dupin.

The theory of evolutionary psychology set out in Poe's earlier works, crudely summarized, is that as relatively inbred bloodlines extend they grow feeble, producing heirs prone to such ills as hypochondria and neurasthenia, and various warped appetites. It was, however, widely taken for granted in the early nineteenth-century that genius and madness were closely allied, and that one could not possibly lay claim to genius without manifesting at least some of these symptoms. The tenor of "The Murders in the Rue Morgue" is not so very different from that of "The Fall of the House of Usher", in spite of the substitution of an eccentric genius for a doomed madman; the principal difference between the characters is, in fact, that Dupin is free to ignore the "superstitions" that have afflicted his rented home, while Roderick Usher had no such luxury.

Having cast himself, imaginatively, in the role of Dupin—which he was to play twice more in fiction, one of the instances, "The Mystery of Marie Roget", being based on an attempt to play the role for real—Poe subsequently felt empowered to test the intuitive limits of his own bipartite soul, first in the "Mesmeric Revelation" and then in the magisterial *Eureka*, which attempted to build contemporary astronomical data into a coherent cosmological model. For Poe, however, this was a gradual process; the road from "Metzengerstein" to *Eureka* was long and winding.

Baudelaire had all this work more-or-less simultaneously available to him, and he had started reading within sight of the road's end. Besides, he had probably started out with a greater faith in his own intuitive genius, and in the essential *utility* of his own mystical inclinations. It is not surprising that he recognized Poe as a kindred spirit; nor is it surprising that he was one of very few people who were able to do so. Poe was eventually to gain other adherents in his own homeland, particularly among the members of H. P. Lovecraft's circle, but the dictates of hindsight had altered his exemplars very considerably by then, and the precise nature of his evolution as a writer and thinker had been thoroughly obscured. Apart from Baudelaire, the only writer of any real magnitude who encountered his work in a fairly fresh condition, and took its lessons very much to heart, was the Comte de Villiers de l'Isle Adam.

Anyone who read Baudelaire's translation of "Berenice" without having previously consulted his version of the "Mesmeric Revelation" would probably have had difficulty finding much evidence therein of "rabid inquisitiveness" or seeing how its interest in "mental disorders" and life-after-death could possibly be linked to "speculative sciences". Baudelaire was, however, right to make that connection, and correct in seeing a reflection of his own rabid inquisitiveness in Poe's work. He did not attempt to draft "speculative science" into his own work—although Villiers did—but he did try to explain himself as a figurative "painter of modern life" informed by a quintessentially modern attitude to the world. One aspect of that modernist attitude was his ability to analyze the decadence of contemporary Paris, and Western civilization as a whole, with a new rigor and objectivity.

Had Baudelaire not died at forty-six he might have done a great deal more, but what might Poe—who died even younger—have done, if only he had found a patron, as Auguste Dupin contrived to do, who was willing to feed him and put a decent roof over his head? *Eureka* would have been a new beginning rather than a swan song, its climactic vision of the inevitable decay and death of entire sidereal systems a mere prelude to a thoroughgoing re-evaluation of the psychology of bold delusion and the dark irony of fate—not to mention the imaginative achievements of which a man might be capable after closing the shutters on the glaring world outside and stuffing himself with all manner of exotic food for thought.

# IX.

## BEYOND NATURALISM

As previously noted, Jean des Esseintes, the protagonist of Joris-Karl Huysmans' *À rebours*, asserts that the prose poem is his favorite form of literature: the "osmazome of art". Although *osmazome* is usually translated nowadays as "essential oil" the term was coined to signify an imagined "savory principle" of flesh that might be obtained in solution by steeping flesh in alcohol. Huysmans was undoubtedly aware of that meaning and employed the term precisely because of its association with the aromatics of flesh.

Des Esseintes has compiled an anthology of prose poetry for his own use, in which Baudelaire's classic exercises are supplemented by contributions from Villiers de l'Isle Adam, Stéphane Mallarmé and Aloysius Bertrand. One name is, of course, diplomatically omitted from this list of significant pioneers of prose poetry: Huysmans' own. The items of that sort he collected in his first book, *Le Drageoir à épices* [The Spice-Box] (1874) and his fourth, *Croquis Parisiens* (1880; expanded second ed. 1886; tr. as *Parisian Sketches*) are particularly interesting, not only in exhibiting the influence exerted on Huysmans by Bertrand and Baudelaire, but also in mapping the transition of his own work from Naturalism to Decadence.

In 1874, Huysmans had been working as a clerk in the Ministry of the Interior for six years, and he was to continue in that occupation for a further twenty-four. He wrote all the books he produced before his retirement—including such scandalous endeavors as *À rebours* and *Là-bas* (1891)—in his office at the ministry, because conditions there were far more suitable than at home. Although his job prevented him from ever descending into genuine poverty, Huysmans retained habits of thrift acquired during a deprived childhood, to which he had been consigned when his father died and his mother married a man named Og, who packed him off to a local boarding school. While working as a clerk he always lived in a squalid part of the *quartier Latin*, in various accommodations that were almost never comfortable and almost always ill-lit. He spent little of his leisure time indoors, wandering the streets relentlessly and haunting the second-hand bookstalls along the *quais*, eventually accumulating an eccentrically eclectic collection of books. The observations he made in the course of his wandering provided the raw material for all his early works.

*Le Drageoir à épices*—whose twentieth-century publishers corrected the deliberate mistake in the title by replacing *à* with *aux*—is a conspicuously immature work, poised uneasily between attempts to cultivate sensory accuracy and stylistic artificiality, but it foreshadows later developments in several interesting ways. Huysmans thought well enough of "Ritournelle"—a brief study of a downtrodden woman, whose title is a musical term referring to tiresome repetition—to reprint it in *Croquis Parisiens*, but he made no such provision for "Extase" [Ecstasy], in which a young man's post-coital reverie is brought down to earth when his lover has to get up to attend to her "vulgar needs". The latter is a deliberate exercise in naturalism, whereas the former attempts to move beyond its limitations: a move not merely encouraged but virtually enforced by the principles of prose poetry.

The longest piece in the book is "Claudine", a cynical subversion of conventional love stories whose heroine is forced to the realization that "men are monsters" because "the more intensely they love, the shorter the time they remain faithful", but marries anyway, for money. Almost as long, however—and more significant, in terms of the subsequent development of the author's work—is a study of "La Rive gauche", which focuses on the Bièvre, one of the streams feeding the Seine from the south, then in the process of being gradually swallowed up by the rapidly-expanding city. When Huysmans used to walk along the Bièvre's course, towards Ivry, it was already heavily polluted, but in "La Rive gauche" he speaks with a certain sentimental affection of its waters, "black with the soot of Paris" and redolent with the odors of "mud and old leather", and he compliments the poplars that line its banks.

Huysmans was working under the influence of the emergent literary school of Naturalism, whose first key exemplars had been provided by the brothers Goncourt—the younger of whom, Jules, died in 1870—but whose principal exponent by 1874 was Émile Zola. Their literary method was already becoming widely known as *Naturalisme*, although Zola did not produce the formal manifesto bearing that title until 1876. By that date, Huysmans had become part of a group of five like-minded writers—the others were Henri Céard, Léon Hennique, Paul Alexis, and Guy de Maupassant—who met for dinner once a week; he completed his first novel, *Marthe, Histoire d'une fille*, in that year, publishing it in Belgium because he was fearful of Napoléon III's censors and the possibility that attention from that quarter might imperil his job.

The ambitious author sent a copy of *Marthe* to Edmond de Goncourt, and persuaded Henri Cérd to introduce him to Zola in order that he could present a copy to the great man personally. With the support of Catulle Mendès, the editor of *La République des Lettres*—to whom Paul Alexis had introduced him—Huysmans persuaded Zola to host the weekly meetings of their expanded circle for a while; the meetings briefly became the social core of the Naturalist movement, although Goncourt—who considered himself and Zola to be poles apart, in social if not in literary terms—remained conscientiously isolated.

It transpired, however, that Huysmans and Zola had less in common with one another than either of them had first assumed. In 1866, Zola had written an account of his own literary tastes—which Huysmans had undoubtedly read, and with which he certainly sympathized—in which he described them as "depraved" and expressed a liking for "literary stews" that were "highly spiced, decadent works in which a sort of aching sensibility replaces the rude health of the classical epochs". That was very much the way Huysmans felt, not merely about literature but about life. Zola had, however, been exaggerating for rhetorical effect; his version of Naturalism conserved far less decadent sensibility than Huysmans' first two Naturalist novels, both of which are narrowly focused on the lives of prostitutes and the route by which poor women are driven to that vocation.

Huysmans would not have been exaggerating at all had he described his own tastes and inclinations in Zola's terms. He never enjoyed "rude health", although he might have fared a good deal better had he ever bought and cooked his own food instead of eating all his meals in restaurants. For many years he condemned himself to suffer in the worst restaurants in the *quartier Latin*—an experience that colors his quasi-autobiographical novel *À vau l'eau* [With the Flow] (1882; tr. as *Downstream*), whose writer-protagonist Folantin is perpetually in quest of a decent meal. Huysmans' own gustatory quest was, however, a little more complicated than that. He continued to frequent terrible eateries even when he was able to afford better ones, extrapolating an aesthetic appreciation of bad food that presumably began as an attempt to make a virtue out of a necessity but eventually became a deliberate exercise in perversity. Ultimately, he was to do the same with ill-health, cherishing the cancer of the mouth he developed in the early years of the twentieth century—which slowly destroyed his jaws, palates and teeth—in the same connoisseur spirit that he brought to his fictionalized biography of the exceedingly agonized martyr *Sainte Lydwine de Schiedam* (1901).

Much more than Zola, Huysmans was also possessed of an "aching sensibility" that he never managed to satisfy. He always suspected that he was unattractive to women, but that was not the real source of his amatory problems. Like his dogged insistence on savoring bad food, his abiding fascination with streetwalkers became a perverse preference rather than a substitute for a more respectable and enduring relationship. Although he did have at least two long-lasting sexual relationships with women who lived with him, both relationships are effaced from his quasi-autobiographical novels; his self-modeled protagonists are always socially isolated and sexually alienated.

Zola opined, when Huysmans followed up *Marthe* with *Les Soeurs Vâtard* (1879), that his disciple's concerns were too narrow for his work to qualify as authentically Naturalistic; what was in them was certainly grimly realistic, but there was far too much of real life left out. When Edmond de Goncourt reviewed the book, he complained that its subject matter had been more than adequately covered already, and that further repetition might seem suggestive of unhealthy obsession. Zola may well have had further reservations about the artificiality of the literary style that Huysmans was now developing by degrees, having returned to the literary territory of *Le Drageoir à épices* much more successfully in the pieces collected in the first edition of *Croquis Parisiens*. The caustic wit typical of *À rebours* (1884) is displayed in advance in this volume, and the overall tone of the book is one of sarcastic black comedy.

The reviews of *Croquis Parisiens* zeroed in on two of its calculatedly scandalous hymn of praise, one celebrating the paradoxical beauty of "L'Ambulante" [The Street-Walker] and the other the perfume of "Le Gousset" [The Armpit]. François Coppée judged them the product of an "unhealthy imagination" and declared that the latter item—the final piece in the first edition—would "permanently relegate the book to the *Enfer* section of public libraries". It is worth observing, however, that both essays are about public displays, not private indulgences; it is the cosmetically-enhanced appearance of the street-walker that Huymans celebrates, and "Le Gousset" is not about individual armpits encountered in intimate circumstances but about the manner in which female armpits exposed *en masse* in summer crowds produce a kind of visual and aromatic symphony.

The more intimate pieces in the first version of *Croquis Parisiens* do not involve women at all, but solitary experiences. The section of the book subtitled *Petits Coins* [Little Corners] leads off with "Ballade en prose de la chandelle des six" [Prose Ballad of the Tallow Candle], which is a parody of stereotyped poems about light but also expresses a genuine fascination with the cheapest available form of domestic lighting—whose inadequate illumination and rank odor Huysmans had conscientiously learned to savor, just as he had cultivated his tastes for poor food, poor health and fallen women. The fact that he found it impractical to write by the light of a tallow candle only increased the piquancy of his appreciation.

The leading item of the *Paysages* [Landscapes] section, "La Bièvre", is even more revealing, especially by contrast with Huysmans' earlier account of the same landscape in "La Rive gauche". "La Bièvre" is also a parody, this time of conventional poetic celebrations of rivers, but there is a similar sincerity in its brutal aesthetic inversions. Here the stream becomes a "moving dung-heap", which emits "a fetid stench of stagnation" and "an aroma of the charnel house"—but it is still given due credit for nurturing poplars. The piece begins with the bald assertion that "Nature is only interesting when it is sickly and desolate"; the other three *Paysages* and the other three *Petits Coins* follow this dictum relentlessly in their descriptions of inner-city decay and creeping urban spoliation. The four other *Types de Paris* who share that section with "L'Ambulante" are the natives of such scenery. Although only one other item, the hallucinatory fantasy "Les Similitudes" [Similarities], shares the *Fleurs de Narines* [Flowers of the Nostrils] section with "Le Gousset", the remainder of the book is by no means ungenerous with its perversely appreciative aromatic references.

By the time that *Croquis Parisiens* was published, Huysmans was hard at work on his third novel, *En ménage* [At Home] (1881), which posts a cautionary signpost for critics enthusiastic to interpret the author's mock-autobiographical novels as accurate reflections of his life, by focusing on the problems of a writer's marriage. *À vau l'eau* is similarly oblique, providing a kind of counterpoint to *À rebours*, whose title labels it as the second component of an opposed pair. Huysmans did not begin work on *À rebours* immediately, though; first he began another Naturalist novel, which aimed—perhaps in response to Zola's criticisms—to present a much broader cross-section of society. It was to have been titled *Gros-Caillou*, that being the name of a dance-hall providing a setting for its key encounters—but he abandoned it, perhaps because he found its diffuse substance far less easy to develop than the tightly-focused narratives of *En ménage* and *A vau l'eau*, but perhaps because the text was already being monopolized by the dance-hall's "tobacco-girls", thus falling into the same obsessive groove as *Les Soeurs Vâtard*. Its first chapter was preserved in the second edition of *Croquis Parisiens*, where it became the longest item.

When he abandoned *Gros-Caillou* to begin work on *À rebours* Huysmans also abandoned Naturalism in order to deal with the substance of gaudy dreams and luxurious desires, projecting his "depraved" tastes into a social milieu of which he had no experience—although his friend Stéphane Mallarmé had the privilege of being acquainted with the flamboyant dandy Comte Robert de Montesquiou, and gladly fed Huysmans' insatiable appetite for rumors of Montesquiou's affectations and extravagances, so that Jean Des Esseintes might adopt the best of them.

The other pieces that Huysmans added to the second edition of *Croquis Parisiens* included several items of spin-off from *À rebours*. The second edition was significantly rearranged, "Le Gousset" being moved to the same section as "Ballade en prose de la chandelle des six", now resubtitled *Fantaisies et Petit Coins*, while the final section, which added two new hallucinatory pieces to "Les Similitudes", was entitled "Paraphrases". The new lead item of this section was "Cauchemar" [Nightmare], a surreal extravaganza inspired by the art-work of Odile Redon. Huysmans, like Baudelaire before him, had become an assiduous art critic, a key promoter not merely of Édouard Manet and the Impressionists who came after him but a fervent champion of the small group of artists whose work became the visual dimension of the Decadent Movement, including Redon, Felicien Rops and—most importantly—Gustave Moreau.

"Cauchemar" is the obvious seed of the nightmare that Des Esseintes experiences after assembling his notorious collection of bizarre plants; it has the same immense focus on hybrid flowers whose buds give rise to abundant images of human female sexuality as well as to such masculine heads as "an old acrobat weeping over his enfeebled loins" and an "ancient lord tormented by spleen". This nightmare's progress, however, extends to extremes even beyond those experienced by Des Esseintes, which were not taken up again until the American writer Clark Ashton Smith took Decadent style and subject-matter to their ultimate. Its final phase takes the dreamer into weird extraterrestrial landscapes reminiscent of "amphitheatres on the moon"; the concluding image is of a desolate planet whose blanched soil nurtures yet more metallic plants with human heads for buds, but here the final head to emerge displays an expression in which "grief merged more ambiguously with the irony of a ghastly smile".

One of the new pieces added to the *Fantaisies et Petit Coins* section—the most numerous in the second edition—is "L'Obsession", dedicated to Edmond de Goncourt. It describes a flight of fancy inspired by an alleged assembly of newspaper advertisements, which also includes some (highly unlikely) solutions to crossword and metagram puzzles. Its reproduction of the kind of nostalgia for the rural provinces that Goncourt and many other Parisian poets habitually affected is blatantly sarcastic; Huysmans loathed the provinces, and rural landscapes in general—especially the south of France (which he never actually visited). This kind of satire was not, however, an experiment that he felt inclined to follow up. Another experimental piece that Huysmans did not follow up is "Damiens", which is arguably the most striking of all the sketches he outlined while slowly getting his head around the substance of *À rebours*. Unlike "L'Ambulante" and "Le Gousset", "Damiens" approaches the subject of prostitution from an intimate and personal—but conscientiously ironic—angle.

Robert Damiens, after whom the piece is titled, had attempted in 1757 to assassinate Louis XV as he got into his carriage at Versailles, with a woefully inadequate dagger (to which Huysmans refers, *en passant* as a "pen-knife"). Although the wound he inflicted was very slight, his judges decided that a deterrent example had to be made of him, so they condemned him to public execution in the most horrible fashion they could imagine; this involved roasting his offending hand over a slow fire, tearing his flesh with pincers, and pouring various hot liquids—including molten lead—into the consequent wounds. The exemplary exercise was concluded by having him torn limb from limb by four horses tugging his body in different directions, but this last operation proved surprisingly difficult to achieve. A pause in the proceedings was required, while levers effected preliminary dislocations—which doubtless helped to maximize the poor fellow's sufferings but detracted somewhat from the theatricality of the climax.

Although the horror of this spectacle attracted the attention of several writers interested in its sadistic exploitation—a dramatization by the German Decadent writer Hans Heinz Ewers can be found in John Gawsworth's anthology *Crimes, Creeps and Thrills*

(1937)—Huysmans evokes the name only to provide a calculatedly absurd analogy with the sensations that the prose-poem's narrative voice feels when purchasing the services of cheap whores. "Had I not morally endured a torture identical with that undergone by the body of the regicide?" that voice asks, disingenuously. "Had I not been torn apart on a spiritual Place de Grève by four different reflections—quartered, as it were: firstly, by thoughts of base lust; then by an immediate disillusionment of my desire as soon as I had entered the room; afterwards by penitential regret at the money spent; and, finally, by the expiatory distress that is always left behind by the fraudulent contracts of the body, once they have been consummated."

This comparison partakes of the same quality of comedy and mockery that is present in so many of the other sketches in the book, but it also has the same underhanded enthusiasm. It is exactly this complex combination of "torments" that the narrative voice seeks in consorting with whores—and one suspects that Huysmans regarded expensive whores in much the same way as expensive restaurants, even when he could afford them. As with tallow candles and promenades along the banks of the Bièvre, he contrived to aestheticize the wretchedness of such experience in such a way that it became superior to, and irreplaceable by, that for which it was supposedly a poor substitute. It is hardly surprising that Émile Zola—who had experienced genuine poverty as an adult, at an extreme that Huysmans never encountered, and was very glad indeed to have escaped it—thought that Huysmans was not a natural Naturalist at all; the evidence provided by *Croquis Parisiens*, even more than that displayed at much greater length in *À rebours* and *Là-bas*, proves the point beyond the shadow of a doubt.

Baudelaire had already expressed the opinion that there could be no *épice* [spice] in love without an element of calculated self-degradation: a *goût du péché* [taste for sin]. Although this is a deliberate perversion of the conventional attitude of the Roman Church to sin, it is also a natural extrapolation of it; if sex is inherently sinful, except for the purposes of legitimate procreation, how can a good Catholic possibly enjoy it by any other means than cultivating a taste for sin? When one bears this in mind, Huysmans' explicit flirtation with Satanism in the researches that produced *Là-bas*, and his subsequent "conversion" become easier to understand. It was only by becoming a good Catholic, having long been a bad one—albeit one who lived for many years in the shadow of Saint-Sulpice and often rented rooms that had one been monastic cells—before he became an even worse one, that he could really reap the perverse rewards of sin.

When he wrote "Damiens", Huysmans was sending up his own inclinations. Although he was never entirely well, his poor health was as moderate in the 1880s as his poverty, and was likewise subject to continual improvement. The pieces of that sort which sprawl upon the pages of *Croquis Parisiens* cannot, however, be dismissed as entirely unserious. When Huysmans did become seriously ill, and began to suffer authentic agony, he refused all recourse to morphia, and gloried in his suffering as he imagined Saint Lydwine to have done, doing his heroic best to cultivate an aesthetic appreciation of its inexorable depredations.

Following his conversion, Huysmans—unlike his books, if one is disposed to agree with Coppée—was presumably not destined for the *Enfer* section of the eternal Library of Souls, but perhaps that ought not to be judged as an entirely happy ending. It is difficult to think of any other man—even among the ill-tempered ranks of doggedly nonconformist writers—who might have found as much in Hell to savor.

# X.

# THE FRUIT OF THE POISONED TREE

Jean Des Esseintes' retreat from Paris, as described in *À rebours*, changes his literary and artistic tastes, causing him to shun, so far as is possible, books and pictures whose subjects are "confined to modern life". For this reason, he begins to prefer the more exotic works of authors he once apparently valued for their realism. The last item in the exemplary list that he offers is his preference for Émile Zola's *La Faute de l'Abbé Mouret* relative to *L'Assommoir*.

This is the only mention of Zola in the novel, and must have seemed a trifle ungrateful to readers familiar with Huysmans' previous prose works, which had been heavily influenced by Zola's work and by the Naturalist manifesto that the author had been stung into compiling by hostile criticism. Given that Des Esseintes takes the trouble to explain his fascination with Charles Baudelaire's poetry at some length, and lavishes several pages of praise on the prose works of Jules Barbey d'Aurevilly, Zola—who undoubtedly read the book—might well have felt short-changed, as he might also have done by Des Esseintes relentless championship of the artificial against the natural. The latter point of principle is a stark contradiction of the allegiance that Zola had eventually formed—though not without difficulty—as a result of chronicling the effects of hereditary corruption on the appalling Rougon-Macquart family.

Had it not been for that particular inversion of allegiance, Zola's Naturalism and Huysmans' revised version of Baudelairean Decadence would not have seemed dissimilar to many critics. Naturalists and neo-Decadents shared a fascination with the seamier side of life—extending from conventional immorality to what Baudelaire had called "the phosphorescence of putrescence"—and they seemed equally "decadent" in both the trivial sense in which the word was used by stern moralists and in the specific literary sense in which the epithet had once been hurled at any Romantic writer who trampled roughshod over the assumptions of Classicism. By the time Zola began chronicling the generations of the Rougon-Macquarts against the background of the Second Empire, Romanticism had become intellectually and aesthetically respectable—of which there was no better proof than the fact that Victor Hugo, exiled from Paris by Napoléon III, stayed away until the Empire fell even after being offered amnesty—and the new literary decadence seemed to be a further phase in literature's headlong fall from Classical grace, in which Naturalist preoccupations with drunkenness and prostitution were at least as much at fault as Baudelariean scabrousness.

It is not surprising that the Rougon-Macquart novel in which Des Esseintes could still find solace in his elective exile is *La Faute de l'Abbé Mouret,* because it is, in some respects, the odd man out in the set of twenty, representing an interesting moment in the moral and intellectual development of the series, at which its dynamic thrust might have veered off to take a different fork in the road to enlightenment. It is no coincidence that the eponymous protagonist of the final volume of the series, who is entrusted with its final summation and the extraction of its moral, *Le Docteur Pascal*—who never uses his surname (Rougon) because he is the only member of the entire family in which the dire hereditary taints of the Rougons and the Macquarts have allegedly contrived to neutralize and cancel one another out—plays a crucial role in *La Faute de l'Abbé Mouret* as the instigator of the experiment that forms the novel's plot. Had that experiment worked out even slightly differently, the conclusions drawn from it in *Le Docteur Pascal* would inevitably have been different, and Zola's own declared conclusion—that Nature is, after all, to be trusted as an existential guide—might have collapsed, thus recruiting him to the Decadent world-view. We now know that he clung fast to his own conviction through thick and thin—but we can also see, as we read the allegorical account of *La Faute de l'Abbé*

*Mouret*, that there was a moment when it must have been a damnably close-run contest.

*La Faute de l'Abbé Mouret* was published in 1874, four years after the collapse of the Second Empire—an event which, as he readily confessed, Zola had not expected when he first conceived the idea of the series, and which had thrown an awkward spanner into the works of the elaborate time-scheme that he had planned out before he began work on it in the late 1860s. The first English translation of the novel bore the slightly coy title of *Abbé Mouret's Transgression*, although it is nowadays better known by the more forthright title of *The Sin of Abbé Mouret*. In fact, though, *faute* has a wider range of meaning in French than any readily-available English equivalent, being capable of implying a lack as well as an offence, and a mere mistake as well as a culpable act. Although the plot of the novel is essentially a replay of the story of Adam's temptation in Eden, it embodies a scrupulous and ambitious attempt to reconstruct the allegory of the Fall of Man, and thus offers a far more complex and heretical analysis of the notion of "original sin" than any simple rendering of *faute* can be expected to imply.

The central character of the novel, Serge Mouret, is a member of the fourth generation of the descendants of Adélaïde Fouque, whose children variously bore the surnames of her husband, Rougon, and her lover, Macquart; specifically, he is the son of the hysteric Marthe Rougon and the maniacal suicide François Mouret. In Serge Mouret, the hereditary taint takes the form of religious mania; he becomes an obsessive ascetic who is so successful in perverting his sexual feelings into ecstatic Mariolatry that he seems to be beyond the reach of temptation. He is appointed curé of the remote rural parish of Les Artaud, all of whose inhabitants bear the same surname because they are all descended from a single patriarch, and who blithely continue their long tradition of casual interbreeding while paying only the slightest mocking lip-service to the Church of which they are supposedly members. The Abbé is not unduly discontented with his lot, even though his stern superior, Frère Archangias, considers the parish to be a borderland of Hell populated by the damned. Abbé Mouret lives meekly and frugally with his animal-loving sister Desirée, in spite of the fact that she is an unrepentant lover of nature, especially of animals, while "to him, Nature presented only snares and abominations; he gloried in maltreating and despising her, in releasing himself from his human slime."

Such rigor has, of course, to be tested, and it is Mouret's cousin, Dr. Pascal, who attempts to loosen him up a little by introducing him to Archangias' arch-enemy, Jeanbernat—known locally as "the Philosopher"—who lives in the lodge of a derelict estate, within whose protective wall a long-dead member of the Ancien Régime once constructed a beautiful ornamental garden known as Le Paradou for a beloved mistress.

The aged Jeanbernat never goes into the old manor house or Le Paradou, whose former luxury is now thoroughly decadent, being content to tend his own humble salad-garden on the other side of the lodge. A young relative delivered by misfortune into his care while still an infant, Albine, has had the run of it while growing up, and regards it as her true home, loving both its faded magnificence and the vigor that a partial return to wilderness has imported into it. Mouret's first glimpse of Albine and Le Paradou precipitates an unanticipated crisis that soon manifests itself as a fever, and Pascal confides him to Albine's care, on the justified assumption that she will have a better chance of nursing him back to health than his own housekeeper or Desirée.

Mouret loses his memory while enfevered, but is by no means restored to a mental state of pristine innocence, and Albine has a difficult time luring him from his sickroom in the house into the magical garden, which he views with dire suspicion. Even when he grudgingly accepts its gorgeously reckless hospitality, he remains fearful of Albine's assertion that there is an even more magical place hidden somewhere within it: a place of true and perfect happiness. Albine helps to restore his physical health, but cannot persuade him to be happy, and his slow surrender to the garden's "soft voluptuousness" is so tormented by fear and resentment that Albine is led to protest to Le Paradou: "If you really love us, why oh why do you make us so miserable!" Although couched in the present tense, the sentence is essentially a complaint addressed to the Creator—here envisaged as an artful but decadent collaboration of Nature and Artifice rather than a paternalistic Jehovah.

Eventually, Albine and Serge do find the place of true happiness—which is, of course, in the shade of a special tree—and there they finally have sexual intercourse. The exotic ambiguity of Le Paradou is briefly triumphant, but the triumph does not last. The suspicious Archangias, who suspects that the lost Abbé is in Le Paradou but dares not enter the garden in order to confirm the hypothesis, finds a gap in the wall and clears away the brushwood with which Albine has carefully blocked it, so that Serge is able to catch a glimpse of Les Artaud—which has the effect of restoring his memory.

As soon as he remembers who and what he is, the restored Abbé becomes acutely aware of the fact that he has not only committed a sin in the eyes of the Church, but has also sacrificed his supposed immunity to temptation. The remainder of the tragedy unfolds with crushing inevitability. Serge becomes Abbé Mouret again, rejecting Albine, who dies of a broken heart; Mouret gives her a Christian burial in spite of the suspicion that she has committed suicide, thus adding compound insult to injury. Jeanbernat's violent but conscientiously restrained revenge on Archangias provides some exceedingly meager moral compensation, but we subsequently discover in the pages of *Le Docteur Pascal*, that Mouret's asceticism never slips again, and that he lives and dies thereafter as the paragon of religious virtue that his corrupt heritage had made of him. The final word of the novel itself is given to Desirée, the true champion of uncaring and unluxurious nature within the story's scheme, and by far the weakest character in the novel.

As an account of the Fall, *La Faute de l'Abbé Mouret* is inevitably complicated by the fact that its Adam cannot be forged from virgin clay, but has to result from a process of erasure. Serge has, in effect, to fall not once but twice; he must fall into innocence before he can fall out of it again, and that proves far more difficult than anyone—certainly not the reader, and perhaps not the author either—could have anticipated. In order to be able to reiterate *Genesis*, the first fall cannot be complete, because Serge has to retain the echo of the prohibition that forbids him to seek the Tree of Life or taste its supposedly-poisonous fruit. That echo of the Church's God blights his mentality in much the same way that parts of Le Paradou are blighted by the more hideous effects of the dereliction into which it has fallen, being given over to repulsive fungi, insects and reptiles.

However healthy, glorious and voluptuous Albine's benign influence can make him, there remains a sector of Serge's soul that is stagnant, putrid and loathsome. That, in fact, is the real poisoned fruit featured in the allegory, not the ecstatic intercourse that he and Albine enjoy—which might have saved him, had he only been a saner and more reasonable man. That, at least, is the way that any sane and reasonable reader would construe the moral of the story, and how Zola evidently intended it to be construed, although admirers of Arcangias—who were probably numerous among the book's original audience—would obviously have taken a different view.

It is easy to see why Jean Des Esseintes liked *La Faute de l'Abbé Mouret* far better than any of Zola's other books, although Joris-Karl Huysmans had not always shared that view. Le Paradou is, in essence, the ideal that Des Esseintes can only try to simulate in a conspicuously meager fashion in the suburbs of Paris—an ideal no less magnificent because it seems to be merely a spoiled relic of a more distant ideal. Unlike a Classicist or wholehearted Romantic, Des Esseintes is wise enough, and sufficiently aesthetically refined, to know that a harmonious compromise of Nature and Artifice is preferable to either absolute. In any case, the greater glories of the *Ancien Régime* are as far beyond his reach as they were beyond the reach of the Second Empire, even in the partly-decayed state in which we find the garden in the novel. Just as Zola sought inspiration for the design of his imaginary garden in the hothouses of the Jardin des Plantes, so Des Esseintes imports exotic botanical specimens into his refuge, and whereas Serge and Albine indulge in heady olfactory orgies that their author generously lays on for them, Des Esseintes does what he can to copy them with the aid of concoctions fabricated by contemporary perfume factories.

Jean Des Esseintes would have delighted in living in Le Paradou, even—perhaps especially—without Albine, and he must have savored the adventure related in the story to the full, appreciating its tragic conclusion as well as anyone. For him, the book qualified as a fabulous exercise in escapism, offering generous temporary solace for his own irredeemably sick soul. He, like any other reader possessed of the Decadent world-view, would have been able to set aside Zola's own conviction—probably half-formed and certainly ill-expressed when he penned this particular text—that nature was ultimately trustworthy in the raw, in order that he might indulge the voluptuousness of Le Paradou's residual artificiality to the fullest possible extent. While reading it, it must have been possible for Des Esseintes to imagine that Zola's career and conviction might eventually work out differently, and that the author might yet be persuaded by the hidden force of his own imagination to relent in his Naturalist faith. *À rebours* was published in 1884, nine years before Zola brought the Rougon-Macquart series to its conclusion in *Le Docteur Pascal*.

It is, in fact, in *Le Docteur Pascal* that the fruit of the poisoned tree designed in *La Faute de l'Abbé Mouret* finally reached maturity, when Zola delivered his final verdict on the problem of heredity and the mysterious ways in which Nature works. The novel has always been regarded as one of the least satisfactory items in the series, but not necessarily for the reasons that Jean Des Esseintes would have considered it unsatisfactory. Some readers thought that it stretched credibility too far—it features, among other exotica, a seemingly efficacious elixir of life made from liquidized sheep's brains and a case of spontaneous human combustion—and others thought that its development of a love affair between an old man and his teenage niece was a trifle distasteful, but Des Esseintes would not have had the least objection to any of that. In his view, the novel's moral failure would have rested not in what its author and protagonist actually did, but in what they did not do: in the text's arrant, craven and lamentable moral cowardice.

The plot of *Le Docteur Pascal* is brutally uncomplicated. The doctor, an alleged scientific genius, has increasing difficulty as he gets older in protecting his carefully-documented but as-yet-unpublished life's work from his mother, Félicité, and his housekeeper, Martine. Both of them want to burn it all—the former because it includes a minute record of the family's hereditary corruption and the latter because her simple religious faith leads her to consider it intrinsically satanic. Pascal's niece and trusted secretary Clotilde is briefly persuaded to help his enemies, resulting in a breach between them, but when he is ruined financially by the chicanery of his banker, Clotilde confesses her love for him and becomes his stoutest defender. Strangely enough, though, Pascal's reaction to his discovery that he is also in love with her is to send her away, leaving himself and his work defenseless—with the ultimate result that all his work does, indeed, go up in smoke, following an untimely death that he refuses to prevent by means of his own elixir of life, on the grounds that nature had better take its course.

Even readers of *Le Docteur Pascal* who have not the slightest sympathy with Félicité's desire to protect her family's reputation or Martine's antiscientific religiosity are bound to regard the loss of the scientist's life's work as a tragedy, but they are also bound to regard the aging Pascal portrayed in the latter chapters of the novel as a complete idiot, so perversely stubborn in his idiocy as to make it seem highly improbable that his younger self ever made such discoveries in the first place.

The key to the mind-numbing stupidity to which Pascal gradually falls prey is, in effect, provided when he and Clotilde visit the place where Le Paradou once was, before it was pillaged and ploughed up, and he tells her the story related in *La Faute de l'Abbé Mouret*. At first, he is wildly enthusiastic about Le Paradou, lavishing praise on the beauty of the garden and Albine, and stating forthrightly that the love that Serge and Albine shared was a "triumph of Life"—but he does that in a sort of hallucinatory rhapsody, and Clotilde brings him back down to earth by asking the crucial question: "Did Serge not love her, then, since he let her die?" Then, releasing the hand he has been holding, Pascal tells her, gnomically, that "things would be too beautiful if men did not spoil them." He says little more to her in answer to her question, but the narrative voice explains his silence as an awareness of the impossibility of paradisal life and an acceptance of "all the stains and blemishes disfiguring humanity." This acceptance is not stoical, however, for Pascal allegedly retains "an admiration for the forces of life" that fills him with a "perpetual delight" and a "fraternal, compassionate tenderness." If the narrative voice were telling the truth on the matter, however, the rest of the story would have worked out very differently.

In fact, the narrative voice is obviously lying at this point in the narrative, or at least deluding itself. Delight and tenderness are as conspicuously missing from Pascal's sentiments and actions throughout the remainder of the text as intelligence; not only does he foul up his own life and legacy, but he does so grimly and harshly. All his prating about the forces of life, and their fine irresistibility, cannot endure in company with his awareness of the essential disfigurement of humankind. At the end of the day, Pascal's conviction that he is free of the Rougon-Macquart taint, by virtue of the gift of "innateness" that has cancelled it out, has to be called into question. Whatever he and the narrative voice allege, his actions demonstrate that he is as mad as any of his relatives, and that, seen as a whole, his two-stage death—first of his flesh and then of his work—is just as obvious a case of spontaneous human combustion as the demise of his alcoholic uncle. He demonstrates, even though he can never quite bring himself to state the fact, that trust in Nature is, in essence, trust in pain and misery, disease and death—none of which is in the slightest regard trustworthy, even if one prefers to represent them all as mere aspects of "the force of life".

If Jean Des Esseintes had had the opportunity to read *Le Docteur Pascal* he would have seen what Pascal Rougon obviously could not, and Émile Zola did not seem to be able to: that Le Paradou really was the glorious creation is appeared to be, which really did harbor a possibility of true happiness, and that Serge Mouret really could and really should have continued to live there with Albine, regardless of the pricking of his crazy conscience. Le Paradou was certainly not paradise, but that is not the point; the point, as Des Esseintes would have known and appreciated, is that only in the artful combination and alliance of the Natural and the Artificial is there any hope at all, not merely for happiness but for progress, not merely for innocence but for virtue, and not merely for humankind but for life itself.

A sheep's-brain smoothie cannot provide an authentic elixir of life, and it was silly of Zola to pretend, even for a moment, that it might; but that does not mean that medical science is impotent, and ought to be abandoned in favor of trust in Nature, and it was even sillier of Zola to imply that the latter might be a better intellectual and moral course to follow. There never was a magical tree in any magical garden whose shade really could provide true happiness, any more than there was ever a magical tree in any magical garden whose forbidden fruit might inform people that they were naked and bring down the utterly unreasonable wrath of an insane God upon their heads; as allegories go, however, Zola's is far superior to that of *Genesis*. It is surely to be regretted that even the author of the earlier novel could not accept its inherent impetus, by allowing Serge Mouret to be content with one fall rather than forcing him to repeat history—as both tragedy and farce—by imposing a second upon him.

Like Pascal Rougon, Émile Zola knew that the worst metaphorical poisonous fruit does not grow on trees, but in our loins. Unfortunately, Zola could not believe—even though he glimpsed the possibility, laid the appropriate allegorical groundwork and actually had Dr. Pascal say as much before his unfortunate lapse into ignominious impotence—that the toxin in question could ever be rendered impotent or harmless. Jean Des Esseintes could not believe that either, but at least he had sufficient intelligence and moral integrity not to try to pretend that the impossibility might be a good thing. The ultimate moral of *À rebours* is, after all, that only the impossible is worthy of commitment, and that the perversity of the hollow gesture of faith is what makes it worthwhile.

# XI.

## MASKED LIVES

The reading-list of modern French literature provided in Joris-Karl Huysmans' *À rebours*—particularly the series of recommendations contained in Chapter XIV—features most of the nineteenth-century's leading writers in that language, but is highly selective in specifying the aspects of their work that recommend them for attention within the Decadent world-view. Jean Des Esseintes has read a great deal, but he has thrown out many of the books he once owned. Balzac, whom he once adored, has been discarded in his entirety for being "too healthy," but the works of other great writers have been filtered according to calculatedly perverse principles, so that certain less celebrated works have been retained while ones that have been more widely applauded have been eliminated.

It is not surprising to find Émile Zola in the group of filtered writers, there being much in his work that could never be accused of excessive health; nor is it surprising that the particular work Des Esseintes praises—by comparison with *L'Assommoir*—is *La Faute de l'Abbé Mouret*. Gustave Flaubert obviously belongs in this group too, *La tentation de Saint Antoine* being manifestly preferable to *L'Éducation sentimentale*. The writer bracketed by these two on the list is, however, far less expectable, not merely because it would be hard to think of anyone with less apparent sympathy for Decadence, but because the two cited texts seem far more similar than the clearly-contrasted items making up the other comparisons. The author in question is Zola's fellow pioneer of the Naturalism that Huysmans had once embraced, Edmond de Goncourt, whose *La Faustin* is favorably contrasted with *Germinie Lacerteux*, the latter being generally considered the best—or, at least, the most influential—of the earlier novels Goncourt had written in collaboration with his younger brother Jules.

The Goncourts are chiefly remembered nowadays for the belatedly-published *Journal* that they kept from 1851 (when Edmond was twenty-nine and Jules twenty-one) until Jules' death in 1870. Edmond continued it thereafter until his own death in 1896, but it was a project far better served by two heads than one. What the journal contained was, in essence, malicious gossip, and malicious gossip is essentially a collaborative project. The Goncourts' tastes and attitudes, as revealed in the *Journal*, were flatly opposed to those of Jean Des Esseintes. They disliked and disapproved of Charles Baudelaire and Paul Verlaine, and affected to despise the Comte de Villiers de l'Isle Adam.

The Goncourts were well aware of the many symptoms of decadence that surrounded them in the Parisian *monde*, and disapproved of them ostentatiously—except, of course, for the ones they happened to manifest themselves. As portentous aesthetes, manic collectors of *objets d'art* and—above all—dedicated neurasthenics, they could very easily have been mistaken for perfect embodiments of the Decadent personality, had they not striven so hard to refuse and repudiate Decadent sensibilities and the Decadent lifestyle; perhaps they would not have tried so hard had they not felt somewhat endangered.

Following Jules' death, Edmond did make one very useful contribution to the as-yet-unhatched Decadent Movement by becoming a significant father-figure to Jean Lorrain, in whom he seemed to find an echo of his dead brother. Goncourt always saw his friendship with Lorrain as a failed mission of salvation, though; he always regretted the fact that Lorrain was prey to literary and sexual predilections that he considered perverse, and cut him out of the will in which he divided his fortune between the writers appointed to form what became known as the Académie Goncourt. The fact that neither Goncourt brother ever married, however, coupled with their flagrant misogyny, rampant neuroses and obsessive devotion to art and literature, encourages the suspicion that the principal difference between Goncourt and Lorrain was the degree of their fastidious denial of their own homosexuality. The same suspicion inevitably attaches to their literary work—that the line separating the insistent moralism of Goncourt's work from the self-conscious sickness of Lorrain's is not as distinct as it might be, given the extent of their mutual fascination with vice and dissolution.

The pattern of the Goncourts' literary career is a striking one. Their early novels were insignificant, their breakthrough work being *Les Hommes de lettres* (1860), in which a potential literary genius is ruined by the nagging of his unappreciative wife and the persecutions of hostile reviewers. This was a topic to which the brothers were to return in *Manette Salomon* (1867), although the narrative viewpoint of the latter work was shifted to bring the female character into the foreground. With only one exception—Edmond's belated account of the circus performers *Les Frères Zemganno* (1879)—all the other novels the brothers penned between 1860 and 1884 place their female characters center-stage. All of them are, in essence, extended character studies, following and extrapolating the highly significant literary precedent set by Flaubert in *Madame Bovary* (1857).

Like Zola's *Thérèse Raquin* (1867), the Goncourt's studies of female "nature" pose as clinical studies; they became foundation-stones of the quasi-scientific school of literary Naturalism. They are not so much exercises in proto-psychology as hypothetical ventures in psychopathology, because they take it for granted that female nature is fundamentally abnormal by comparison with the male norm. The modern reader, looking back at the novels from a standpoint that can hardly take such an assumption for granted, is far more likely to see pathological tendencies in the behavior of the male characters who abuse the central characters at the authors' behest, but none of the leading Naturalists doubted their own objectivity or perspicacity. Few of their contemporary readers, of either sex, could have seen anything unnatural or inexcusable in the behavior of the men who bring about the ruin of the eponymous characters.

The Goncourts' earliest studies of female psychology, *Soeur Philomène* (1861) and *Renée Mauperin* (1864), are ostentatiously sympathetic to their heroines. The former, having been brought up in unfortunate circumstances, has no opportunity to reap the conventional rewards of life, and can only succeed in becoming virtuous by exceedingly rigorous self-denial. The latter, being far more comfortable in her social situation, follows an opposite existential trajectory, carelessly losing the innocence that is her birthright and moving inexorably towards the miserable death that is, in this kind of fiction, the inevitable wages of sin.

*Germinie Lacerteux*, which followed hot on the heels of *Renée Mauperin*, was based on the story of one of the Goncourts' own servants, Rose Malingre, who contrived to maintain an appearance of docile respectability in the household, although the aftermath of her death brought to light a very different life outside it. The excesses of Germinie Lacerteux's secret life of drunken debauchery and congress with her two predatory lovers are probably exaggerated by comparison with Rose Malingre's, but the exaggeration presumably provides accurate testimony to the shock the brothers received when they realized the extent to which their employee's slavish devotion had been a mere mask. The novel does, however, represent Germinie's precipitous descent of a slippery slope—which leads, via promiscuity, hysteria, alcoholism and crime, to an ignominious demise—as the consequence of early sexual abuse rather than any innate disposition.

The extensions of this sequence in the play *Henriette Maréchal* (1865), *Manette Salomon* and *Madame Gervaisais* (1869) became gradually less sympathetic to their female leads, the last-named providing a harsh case-study in religious hysteria that contrasts sharply with *Soeur Philomène*. (Females, of course, could not sublimate their flawed desires by becoming obsessed with the arts—George Sand, of whom the Goncourts disapproved thoroughly, seemed freakish even to herself—but the convent doors were always open.) One might almost be tempted to conclude that the Goncourts had been psychologically scarred by the treason of their servant, were the hypothesis not so blatantly absurd.

A long interval separated *Madame Gervaisais* from Edmond's unaided additions to the sequence, *La Fille Élisa* (1877), *La Faustin* (1882) and *Chérie* (1884). All three seem a trifle confused by comparison with the earlier works of the same kind, although the first tries hard to recover the spirit of *Germinie Lacerteux* in its account of a prostitute condemned to prison, but Jean Des Esseintes was certainly right to single out *La Faustin* as the most interesting of the three. It is by far the most confused of them, the author having completely lost control of his enterprise. It is the most honest of all the Goncourts' novels—they could never have written it together, while submitting to one another's censorious gaze—and by far the least healthy, not by virtue of having sick subject-matter, but by virtue of the manner in which the subject-matter wrested itself feverishly from the author's grip.

Huysmans was not the only Decadent to observe the fascinating quality of *La Faustin*. Edmond Gourmont's protégé, Jean Lorrain, quotes a key passage from it in a story called "Dolmancé," which is a study in sadism. Dolmancé is a character in the Marquis de Sade's classic dialogue *La philosophie dans la boudoir*, but the argument of Lorrain's story is that sadism is a typically English vice, and his character reads from *La Faustin* in order to provide an archetypal image of the aristocratic English sadist.

The passage Lorrain quotes translates as follows:

> "What, in essence, is your friend Selwyn?"
>
> Lord Annandale, occupied in lighting his cigar and taking a leisurely puff, looked his mistress full in the face and said:
>
> "George Selwyn...is a sadist." And under the mute interrogation of la Faustin's eyes, he exclaimed: "Yes, a man who has the desires and appetites of a deranged and morbid sensuality...But what is it that you...what is his life to us?" And as he began to walk across the room, he mumbled; "A great...a very great intelligence...immense knowledge...and an old childhood friend."
>
> A silence followed.
>
> "Are you going out today Juliette?" he said, after a few moments.
>
> "No!"

On hearing that, Lord Annandale headed for the stables."

(There is no point in English readers hunting for this passage in G. F. Monkshood and Ernest Tristan's 1906 translation of *La Faustin*, where it is comprehensively bowdlerized; it is not just that the references to sadism and morbid sensuality are omitted, but that Annandale's obvious embarrassment and Juliette's shocked response are smoothed over, making the exchange utterly anodyne—thus condemning the reader to total bewilderment as to the reasons for the conversation's dark aftermath.)

The Decadent qualifications of *La Faustin* do not derive from the inclusion within it of George Selwyn, who appears for the first time a few pages before the end, in order to provide a blatant *deus ex machina*—an abrupt invocation entirely in keeping with the intractable awkwardness that has overtaken the text by this point. The novel's own implicit Decadence—whose triumphant authenticity stands in stark contrast to the author's affectations—is embodied in the character for who the book is named, and in the manner in which she eludes her creator's attempts to pin her down as a specimen and subject her to corrosive moral condemnation. As in the moralistic classic that so inspired Baudelaire, Charles Sainte-Beuve's *Volupté* (1834), the novel's protagonist contrives to escape the author's attempts at censure—a feat all the more remarkable because Juliette Faustin is female. Saint-Beuve's Amaury always had the advantage that his appetites were masculine, and hence natural; Juliette had, at least in her own era, to labor under the handicap of being implicitly undeserving of any such concession.

Juliette is an actress—usually defined more narrowly as a *tragedienne*—who is, as the novel opens, preparing to open at the Théâtre Française in the title-role of *Phaedre* (in Racine's revision of Euripides' original). Her own situation has little enough in common with the wife of Theseus, who secured her damnation when she became infatuated with her stepson, but the author insists in reading abundant premonitions of her own eventual downfall in her conscientious attempts to get to grips with the part. As an actress, Juliette is also a kept woman; her career in the theatre has been—and still is—entirely dependent on her ability to cultivate powerful friends in the "green room" of the theatre. She has been so successful in her seductions that she has outshone the older sister, Maria, who first led her into this immoral way of life, but her very success has led to her becoming far more cynical than her role model—a cynicism that seems even more intensely-realized in the third of the sisters, Lillette, who is only just emerging from childhood (and soon vanishes from the story).

While Maria—who is usually referred to either as "Carsonac's mistress" or by her nickname, Bonne Âme—seems quite happy with her keeper, Juliette has very mixed feelings about hers, a man named Blancheron. So far as the reader can gather, Blancheron seems a decent sort, but he hardly ever appears in person. On the one occasion when Juliette actually seeks him out, having suffered a random pang of affection, she misses him at home and then again at the fencing-school to which he has gone—whereupon she underlines the essential fickleness of her passions by offering herself to the lustful fencing-master, and then abruptly changing her mind and fighting him off. Apart from a couple of self-effacing jokes, Blancheron's only substantial declaration in the story is the suicide note he sends to Juliette when she ditches him, detailing his intention to have himself torn in two by railway trains passing one another as they travel in opposite directions.

Juliette's abandonment of her protector is not quite as callous as this incident—or her casual dismissal of its significance—suggests, for her entire career as a courtesan has been shadowed by her memory of a young Englishman, William Rayne, whose enduring love for her has been deliberately and firmly obstructed by his father. Soon after the novel begins, Juliette finds grounds to suspect—but cannot bring herself to confirm—that Rayne has been killed in India following an encounter with a "black tiger," so it is all the more surprising when he reappears on the eve of a performance, having just inherited his dead father's title. His presence in the audience allows her to enhance her mastery of her role and to complete the sensation she has already caused.

Juliette's reunion with Rayne, now Lord Annandale, is magnificently joyous; they set up house together and are magnificently happy. All her problems—which have been detailed at great length, particularly in the context of a lavish dinner-party in which all the decadence of contemporary Parisian society is sarcastically displayed—are solved. The resolution of her existential predicament is, however, a terrible problem for the author, because no such thing can be allowed to happen within his moralistic framework. It is implicit in the enterprise that Juliette—who is after all, a bad girl—must be ruined, rendered utterly desolate if not actually condemned to a horrible death. In order to achieve this end, Goncourt is forced to go to extreme, and frankly incredible, lengths.

The surprising thing is, of course, that Goncourt ever allowed himself to get into such a mess in the first place. He obviously cannot have intended to write himself into a corner, but he evidently felt that he could not take the easy way out once he had, by simply throwing away some of what he had done. This was not mere laziness; he must have been determined to preserve the text that had delivered him into his quandary because it meant too much to him; he had poured himself into it, because it felt so right while he wrote it, even though it was so obviously wrong within the scheme of his story.

The real heart of *La Faustin* is the dinner-party scene, which occupies chapter sixteen—the longest chapter in the book, and one that comes almost exactly half way through the text, although the chapter numbers eventually extend to a remarkable fifty-five. The conversation is clearly based on the literary dinners that the Goncourt brothers had attended in the 1860s, and many of the anonymous conversationalists are presumably real people whose names have been omitted, in order to take the edge off the sarcastic reportage of their posturing. What is primarily important about the scene, however, is not what is done or said but the fact that it leaves Juliette so completely cold, locked in an impregnable indifference. The next morning, she awakes in a deep depression, sickened by an utter incapacity to engage herself with any aspect of life—a state of mind that the Monkshood/Tristan translation renders quite accurately as "black, intense and splenetic *ennui*."

Juliette can find only one means of releasing herself from this mood, and that is to immerse herself in a book—not *any* book, but a very particular text that has the power to transport her into an exotic world of disorder, anachronism and the supernatural: Thomas De Quincey's *Confessions of an English Opium-Eater*. Some modern readers might suspect Goncourt of excessive diplomacy, and might be disposed to wonder whether he is making an encoded suggestion that Juliette is a habitual laudanum-drinker herself, but that would be a mistake. During the party scene—probably for the first time in the writing of the novel—the author had begun to identify with his character; her poisonous *ennui* is, if not an accurate representation of Goncourt's, at least something he can understand entirely: something into which he can project himself, as fully as an author can.

Although there had been earlier warning-signals, it was this abruptly-cemented identification that carried *La Faustin* decisively astray. Small wonder that it immediately prompted the assertion—far truer of the author than the character as so far described—that the only viable escape from black *spleen* is escapist reading, but then delivered the author into an extraordinarily self-indulgent dream of a truer escape. The impossibly beautiful William is miraculously redeemed from the claws of the black tiger, gifted to Juliette (and thus to the author) in order that both of them might briefly break free of the prison constructed by the text.

It is not in the least surprising that Goncourt was unwilling simply to tear up and throw away the passages of his work that had delivered him into a narrative *impasse*; they were probably the most precious pages he had ever penned. Nor is it surprising that expert Decadent readers like Jean Des Esseintes and Jean Lorrain recognised in *La Faustin* a book in which the most careful author in France—a neurotic paragon of insistent anti-Decadent moral health—had succumbed to his secret malaise, and surrendered to the essential perversity of his own creativity.

It could not last, of course. Goncourt kept the text in which he had betrayed himself, but he could not let it stand as a narrative outcome. Juliette could not possibly be allowed a permanent redemption, even if Goncourt had been able to maintain his identification with her beyond a delicious interlude. Her dream had to be blighted, however absurd the agent of its infection and destruction might now require to be.

Goncourt casts about for a means of destroying La Faustin from within, in a strange sequence of short chapters in which he sets off time and time again to analyze the flaws of her character and make them fatal, but fails. All he can contrive in that direction is to make her refuse her lover's offers of marriage (because she feels unworthy) and force her to retire from the stage, even though she knows that it will reduce her status in his estimation. By the time the plot has reached this point, Goncourt is all too keenly aware that the narrative fault is not in his heroine but in the gift that he has presented to her: the lovely Lord Annandale. It is he, not she, who must be comprehensively spoiled; it is for that purpose that George Selwyn is suddenly and arbitrarily introduced into the plot.

Selwyn makes only one substantial speech, but that is a small masterpiece of symbolism—quite alien to Goncourt's Naturalism—in which he refuses to accept a bottle of smelling-salts from Juliette's hand, because he suffers from a peculiar nervous disorder that causes his hand reflexively to drop any precious object placed therein. The superficially-veiled reference of this remarkable statement is to the relationship between Annandale and la Faustin, which proceeds rapidly to its catastrophic climax, but the sensitive reader might also liken it to Edmond Goncourt's dealings with his own creations.

All authors are, of course, committed sadists; the construction of a plot is, in essence, the careful arrangement of the sufferings to be inflicted upon various characters. Decadent writers not only know this, but revel in it; the rest take refuge in the notion of "poetic justice," which asserts that the good are made to suffer only so that the reader may rejoice in their eventual redemption, while the bad are allowed to prosper only in order that the reader might take legitimate delight in their eventual agonization and humiliation. In all his previous books, Edmond Goncourt had been a steadfast supporter of poetic justice, and a firm believer in its moral healthiness, but in *La Faustin* he faltered.

In the final scene of *La Faustin*, while Lord Annandale lies delirious on the deathbed to which he has been unceremoniously consigned by the long-repressed passions reawakened by George Selwyn, he screams at his loyal servants, ordering them to turn "that woman" out: to dispossess Juliette of her brief salvation. No one in the world could possibly believe, if only for an instant, that there is any justice in this instruction—and no one in the world could believe, for more than an instant, that even Edmond Goncourt could possibly imagine that there is. When Juliette goes to kiss the stricken Annandale, in the hope of restoring his sanity, he thrusts her back violently, accusing her of being nothing but an artist, incapable of love. That is a charge of which Juliette is clearly innocent, in spite of all the sly and malevolent attempts her author has made to incriminate her; if Edmond Goncourt felt the awful force of that accusation, he did so on his own behalf, not hers, and must have known what a terrible indictment it was.

## XII.

## THE NEXT BEST THING

When Jean Des Esseintes recorded the lists of his favorite reading in *À rebours* (1884) he lavished extravagant praise on the Comte de Villiers de l'Isle Adam's short stories, which sent him into raptures of delight. "In this realm of biting, straight-faced satire," he opined, "no other book existed in France. The next best thing was a story by Charles Cros, "La Science de l'amour" [The Science Of Love], originally published in the *Revue du Monde Nouveau*, which was calculated to astonish the reader with its chemical extravagance, its sardonic humor and its icy comic observation—but the pleasure it gave was only relative, for it was fatally defective in its execution. Villiers' style—solid, colorful and often original—had disappeared, to be supplanted by a kind of sausage-meat scraped from the slab of some literary pork-butcher."

Des Esseintes was, of course, no slouch when it came to backhanded compliments or damning with faint praise, but this judgment is extraordinary in its double-edged quality. No other writer is cited in the catalogue for a single short story—along with a (useless) reference to its original place of publication—and none is cited only to have the boot put into him so rudely. What on Earth, one is inclined to wonder, did Joris-Karl Huysmans have against Charles Cros? And why, if he did have something against him, did he bother to mention him at all? Cros was still notorious in literary Paris, at the time this passage was penned, as a man who had once tried to strangle Anatole France in a dispute over a woman—France subsequently blackballed Cros from the third Parnassian showcase anthology and undoubtedly bad-mouthed him at every possible opportunity—but Huysmans barely knew France when he wrote À rebours, and had no inkling of the fat that he would ultimately become the most famous writer in the land. He undoubtedly had infinitely more sympathy for poor Villiers, who was a close friend of Cros for some time, and collaborated with him on several works of art whose nature did not permit their preservation.

Indeed, circumstances dictated that almost all of Cros's endeavors would prove evanescent, and he left far fewer achievements behind him than he had once hoped, but he was at the very heart of the Decadent Movement while it was still in embryo, and would doubtless have featured far more prominently after its birth had he not been so wholehearted a Decadent that he drank himself to death before it really got off the ground, thus becoming one of its lost geniuses. Alas, his published works were not collected until 1954—they required further augmentation, courtesy of the assiduous literary archaeology, before they were as complete as possible, in a further edition of 1964—and no biography appeared until 1969, when Minard published Louis Forestier's *Charles Cros, l'homme et l'oeuvre*. The tale told by Forestier is a harrowing one, itself replete with delicate Decadent touches.

Charles Cros was the youngest of three brothers. Their father, Henri Cros, who was born in 1803, was an excellent but eccentric scholar, who had obtained a doctorate in law but scorned the bar in order to devote his attention to literature and philosophy, making his living as a schoolteacher. By the time Charles was born in 1842, however, his only remaining pupils were his own children, of whom he eventually had four, the others being Antoine (1835-1903), Henriette (1838-1924), and Henry (1840-1907). Henri Cros had published the first edition of his intended masterpiece, *Théorie de l'Homme intellectuel et moral* [The Intellectual and Moral Theory of Humanity], in 1836, and had issued a revised edition in 1838, but it was never taken seriously by his contemporaries and its political and religious opinions made it difficult for him to find gainful employment, even after the revolution of 1848, in which he actively involved himself on the Republican side.

Although Antoine, having rebelled against his father's offbeat idealism by espousing a rigorous materialist philosophy, went on from his home-schooling to study medicine and to launch a very successful medical practice in Paris in 1857, Henry and Charles found it more difficult to adapt to the "real world". As children they played at being publishers, producing title-pages for books that they one day hoped to write, undertaking experiments in the deployment and reproduction of color that became lifelong concerns; Charles labored for many years as an unsung pioneer of color photography and Henry became an artist—he exhibited in the 1863 *Salon des Réfuses*—who did equally pioneering and equally unsung work in colored wax and stained glass. Their education paid particular attention to ancient languages—Hebrew and Sanskrit as well as Greek—philosophy and the arts. When they had to find work, however, they found this training unhelpful and had to amend their ambitions, at least temporarily.

At the age of eighteen Charles obtained a position at the Institution des Sourd-Muets [Institute for Deaf-Mutes], which offered the opportunity to obtain the seeming security of civil service employment; he passed the civil service entrance exam at the end of 1860 and was awarded a salary of 600 francs at the end of 1861. By that time, however, he had been joined by Henry, and the brothers soon began to neglect their work in favor of other joint pursuits; Henry was expelled for dueling in 1863 and Charles was suspended soon afterwards for persistent absenteeism. Charles then started to study medicine, but never finished his studies, although he assisted Antoine during the cholera epidemic of 1865 and again during the Commune in 1871.

Antoine had become a highly fashionable physician in the early 1860s and was also an habitué of several prestigious salons, to which he began taking his younger brothers. The three became sufficiently conspicuous to figure, rather colorfully, in Catulle Mendès' *roman à clef* of Second Empire salon society *La Maison de la Vieille* (1894) as the Kramm brothers. Mendès novel also features an eccentric salon hostess named Stella d'Hélys, whose model was Nina de Villard—the temptress whose flirtation with Anatole France excited Charles Cros to violence.

Charles lived a Bohemian existence for some years, torn between the possibilities of a literary career and a career as an inventor; as well as conducting experiments in color photography, he attempted to develop an "autographic" telegraph system, for which he applied for a patent in 1866. Among the salons to which Antoine introduced him was Camille Flammarion's, which was patronized by a peculiar mix of scientists, publishers, journalists, actors, artists and occultists. Paul Verlaine was a regular there, as well as at Antoine's own salon, and he and Charles became good friends. It may well have been Verlaine who introduced Charles to Nina de Villard's salon in 1868, where Villiers de l'Isle Adam was the resident star. Nina was by no means exclusive in her choice of lovers, but Charles soon became her favorite, and the two entered into a long intimate association.

Nina had been born 1843 as Nina Gaillard, and had married Comte Hector de Callias, an amateur man of letters and an exceedingly heavy drinker, in 1864. When they separated in 1867—they never divorced—Nina kept the title of Comtesse but adopted her mother's maiden name in order to embark on a new life as a socialite. Her salon was conspicuously *avant garde*, entertaining many Parnassians, Wagnerians and political radicals; she was especially fond of putting on performance pieces, in which Villiers routinely starred. The salon's regulars included François Coppée, Catulle Mendès, Jules Richepin and Augusta Holmes as well as Verlaine and Villiers. Not everyone approved of its affections and excesses; the Goncourts described it in their journal as "l'atelier de détraquage cérébral" [the mental-breakdown factory].

Camille Flammarion's infinitely more sober salon hosted a lecture series, to which Cros was invited to contribute a talk—on the possibilities of interplanetary communication using light signals—in May 1869. The paper was subsequently submitted the Académie des Sciences and published in *Cosmos* before being reissued as a pamphlet. That first publication was rapidly followed by an article on color photography, but Cros also made his debut as poet in 1869. He and Nina were both admitted to the second showcase of the *Parnasse contemporain* in that year, before Cros attempted to strangle

France for trying to steal Nina's affections, but it was delayed by the Franco-Prussian war and did not appear until 1871.

The war, which began in July 1870, disrupted both aspects of Cros's nascent career; in December the house where he was still living with his parents was destroyed by a shell-burst. Henri took his wife and daughter south, while Charles moved in with Madame Mauté, Mathilde Verlaine's mother. Mathilde and Mme. Mauté were both Antoine Cros's patients, and were very grateful to him for having nursed them both through smallpox. Cros read the poems that Arthur Rimbaud sent to Verlaine not long thereafter, and went with Verlaine to meet the train on which Rimbaud was scheduled to arrive in Paris, famously missing him. Although more sympathetic to Rimbaud than most of Verlaine's horrified friends, Cros eventually fell out with him—but not until Cros had become a leading light of the Vilains Bonhommes, the literary group that temporarily formed around Rimbaud and Verlaine. When Verlaine and Rimbaud ran away together in July 1872, Cros inevitably sided with Mathilde and her mother, but Verlaine's absence left a gap in his life.

Because of their efforts in lending medical aid to the victims of the uprising, Antoine and Charles were both denounced as Communards, but Antoine had too many influential clients for the charge to stick. Nina, on the other hand, had entertained too many leading Communards in her salon to feel safe, and she fled to Geneva. Charles followed her into exile, and did not return to Paris until April 1873—which did not help his attempts to pick up his interrupted careers, although he did his best to do so at a distance. He continued to publish poems, and also submitted a treatise on *Mécanique cérébrale* [Cerebral Mechanics] to the Académie in May 1872. His first short story "Drame interastral" [An Interastral Drama] was published in *La Renaissance littéraire et artistique* in 1872, and his first collection of poetry, *Le Coffret de santal* [A Sandalwood Casket], in 1873. In March 1874 he launched the *Revue du Monde Nouveau* in collaboration with Henri Mercier; its first issue featured Théodor Banville, Stéphane Mallarmé, Charles Leconte de Lisle, Villiers de l'Isle Adam and Émile Zola. Alphonse Daudet appeared in the second, along with "La Science de l'amour", but the third issue proved to be the last.

Cros wrote a comedy in the vein of Beaumarchais entitled "La Machine à changer le charactère des femmes" [A Method of Changing the Character of Women] for performance in Nina's salon in 1875—Villiers played the other leading part—and collaborated with Nina on another play "Le Moine bleu" [The Blue Monk], which was likewise never performed anywhere else. 1876, his omission from the third *Parnasse contemporain* undoubtedly hurt him, but he achieved his first significant success when some monologues he had written for the salon were reproduced on stage by the actor Ernest Coquelin, who was known as Coquelin *cadet*, to distinguish him from his brother. The most popular was *L'Hareng saur* [The Salted Herring], and Nina hung the ceiling of her drawing-room with salted herrings in commemoration of it.

Cros was not yet done with the other aspect of his work; in 1877 he obtained financial support from the Duc de Chaulnes to continue his work on color photography, and in April of that year he sent a sealed description of a "paleophone" to the Académie des Science; he built a prototype but could not obtain funds to develop it and was overtaken when Thomas Edison filed for a French patent for his near-identical phonograph eight months later. Cros took the disappointment hard, and his troubles were amplified by a terminal split with Nina de Villard, occasioned by his decision to marry a neighbor, Mary Hjardemaal. To make matters worse, he got into a dispute with Coquelin *cadet* over payment for the monologues with which Cros was supplying him, for which the actor was paying a pittance while making a fortune.

In 1879 things began to look up, with the birth of Cros's son Guy-Charles (who went on to become a poet of some note) and the publication of a second edition of *Le Coffret de santal*, but his attempts to develop an acid-free battery came to nothing. He became a prominent member of Émile Goudeau's literary society, the Hydropathes (the name, which signifies a pathological hatred of water, was derived from the inversion of a pun on its founder's name, construed as "goût d'eau"), the meetings of which became a replacement of sorts for Nina's salon. There Cros formed a close friendship with Alphonse Allais, with whom he began to do impromptu performance pieces similar to those he had earlier done with Villiers.

He composed the "Chant des Hydropathes" [Song of the Hydropaths], an anthem to all kinds of hard liquor, which the members delighted in singing while drunk. The society became too large and was suspended in 1880, when its journal *L'Hydropathe* was transformed into *Tout-Paris*, but when Rodolphe Salis founded the literary café Le Chat Noir at the end of 1881 he asked the core membership to reform and meet there; Cros's association with Allais was further developed there, and the two began writing a series of surrealistic *contes sens dessus dessous* (upside-down tales) for *Gil Blas* under the pseudonym Carlemyll; it was, unfortunately, soon aborted.

Although Cros initially declined to involve himself with the journal *Le Chat Noir* when it was founded in 1882, he could not stay away from it for long, and became one of its co-editors in April 1883; he was also involved with *Le Rapin* and, more importantly in hindsight, but abortively, with the founding in the café of a new putative movement of "Zutistes". Its intended showcase, *L'Album Zutique*, did not appear at the time but was eventually published as a curio; its contents included work by Camille Pelletan, Jean Richepin, André Gill and Paul Bourget as well as Cros. As usual, however, Cros's finest work remained transient; Gabriel Astruc's *Le Pavillon des fantômes* (1929) recalls Cros and Allais improvising sketches parodying Jules Verne and Albert Robida "avec une profusion et un cachet d'authenticité stupéfiants" [in profusion, and with an amazing veneer of authenticity].

In 1884—the year in which Huysmans published *À rebours*—Nina de Villard died, a drink-addled wreck; Hector de Callias allegedly turned up to the funeral, but slipped away again, leaving Cros to deliver the eulogy. Cros was, by then, well on his way to joining her, and must have been aware of the fact.

Jean Des Esseintes' comments on "La Science de l'amour" did produce some protests—Remy de Gourmont went out of his way to describe the story as a "masterpiece" in 1891—but Paul Verlaine found no place for Cros in his celebration of *Poètes maudits*, which provided the Decadent Movement with its other principal foundation-stone. In all probability, Verlaine—who was cobbling together a book in order to produce something publishable rather than producing a definitive study—meant no insult by the exclusion of his old friend, but it is possible that he still harbored some resentment over the fact that Cros had taken the side of his wife and mother-in-law during the scandal of 1872.

In 1885, Cros, who was still co-editing *Le Chat Noir*—where he reprinted "La Science de l'amour" in apparent reaction to Huysmans' mention of it—also became involved in the founding of two further periodicals, *Le Scapin* and *La Décadence*, but his fondness for absinthe had taken too heavy a toll and he was no longer in a fit condition to make much contribution to their development. He eventually died on 9 August 1888, after a rapid onset of "phthisis", leaving nothing to his heirs but debts.

Did "La Science de l'amour" deserve the insults that Des Esseintes hurled against its style—and, for that matter, did it deserve any mention at all as a addendum to a celebration of the work of Villiers de l'Isle Adam? Although Villiers's short stories are nowadays hailed as the archetypal *contes cruels*, it was not so much their ironic twists as their satirical humor that recommended them to Des Esseintes, and "La Science de l'amour" is definitely in the same vein. Oddly enough, however, the "style" about which Des Esseintes complains is an essential artifact of the story, and its true subject-matter, being a parody of scientific reportage and the supposed rationality and objectivity of the scientific attitude. The narrator begins by explaining that:

> "While still very young, I had a fine fortune and a taste for science—but not the airy, pretentious science that believes it can create a world entire and leaps into the blue atmosphere of the imagination. I have always thought, in accord with the tightly-organized cohort of modern scientists, that man is merely a recorder of brute facts, a secretary of palpable nature; that the truth, conceived not in a few vain generalizations, but in an immense and confused volume, is only partially accessible by scrapers, clippers, ferreters, porters and warehousers of actual, observable and undeniable facts—in a word, that it is necessary to be an ant, a mite, a rotifer, a bacterium or any-

thing at all, to transport one's atom into the infinity of atoms that comprise the majestic pyramid of scientific truths. To observe and observe, and, above all, never to think, dream or imagine: that is the splendor of present-day method.

"It was with these sound doctrines that I entered into life, and as soon as I had taken my first steps, a marvelous project, a genuine scientific windfall, came to mind.

"When I learned physics, I said to myself: people have studied gravity, heat, electricity, magnetism and light; the mechanical equivalent of these forces has been or will be determined incontestably in a rigorous fashion—but all those who are working on the expression of these elements of future knowledge are only playing a paltry role in society. There are other forces that sagacious and patient observation ought to submit scientific intelligence. I shall not offer a general classification, because I consider them harmful to study and I have no such intention. In brief, I was led—how or why I do not know—to undertake a scientific study of love."

Following that prospectus, the story goes on to describe how the narrator, having taken methodological advice from Frédéric Chopin and Alfred de Musset, causes a young woman—aptly named Virginie—who feels claustrophobically trapped in her parents' home to fall in love with him. He proceeds to seduce her into eloping with him, so that he can install her in a love-nest equipped with countless clandestine measuring devices, in order to monitor all the physiological transformations she undergoes while in the throes of passion:

"In the room where, intoxicated by love, she abandoned herself to my fictitious transports—for I had no time to waste—it was as if we were in a retort. The copper-lined walls prevented any connection with the atmosphere and the air was analyzed rigorously, first as it came in and again when it went out. Potash solutions contained in flasks revealed to skilful chemists on an hourly basis the quantitative presence of carbon dioxide. I remember curious figures in this regard, but they lacked the precision justly required by tabulation, since my own non-amorous respiration was mingled with Virginie's genuinely amorous respiration. Let it suffice for me to mention the large excess of carbon dioxide during those tumultuous nights when passion attained its maxima of intensity and numeric expression.

"Strips of litmus paper cleverly distributed in the linings of her garments revealed the constantly acidic reaction of sweat. Then, on the following days and nights, there were figures to record relating to the mechanical equivalent of nervous contractions, the quantity of tears secreted, the composition of the saliva, the variable hygroscopy of the hair, the tension of anxious sobs and sensuous sighs!

"The results of the *kissometer* were particularly curious. The instrument, which is my own invention, is no larger than the apparatus that Punch-and-Judy men put in their mouths to make their puppets speak, which are known as 'whistles'. As soon as the dialogue became tender and the situation was established as opportune, I put the primed apparatus—covertly, of course—between my teeth."

All goes relatively smoothly until the narrator progresses to the later chapters of his projected study, on "The Effects of Absence and Regret" and "The Mechanics of Chagrin". Although he is entirely successful in inducing the required responses, the regret and chagrin in question manifest themselves in an unfortunate manner when Virginie finds out about the experimental program. She burns all his research notes as well as trashing all his equipment, leaving him with no results to publish—and, the reader is plausibly invited to believe, with no more authentic understanding of the phenomenon of love than he had to start with. The narrator notes:

> "And as I wandered through those empty rooms, I felt—the final mockery of fate—regret for Virginie's flight! Yes, I regretted the loss of that woman more than that of my finest works! And I went to lose consciousness—O shame!—burying my face in my pillow to recover the scent of the tresses that I would no longer be able to touch.
>
> "To cap it all, missing the opportunity to record the analytical elements of such profound heartbreak—such a particular set of violent sensations—I did not think of hitching myself up to the cardiograph!"

Hopefully, with the aid of these translated passages, the readers of the present text will be able to come to their own conclusions about the justice or otherwise of Des Esseintes' criticisms of its baroque style, but one thing, I feel sure, will be apparent: that the story is, indeed, a worthy companion-piece to Villiers' satirical pieces, and does, in fact, encapsulate certain aspects of the Decadent world-view. It is breezily cynical, calculated in its artifice, and deftly perverse, embodying a spirit of flamboyant mockery that became one of the Movement's characteristic tones. It is, admittedly, at the flippant end of the Decadent spectrum, although not as close to the terminus of the spectrum as the proto-surrealist "upside-down tales" that Cros was later to write in collaboration with Alphonse Allais. Indeed, looking back at Cros's career, one is bound to wonder what might have become of Allais had he continued his double act with Cros in Le Chat Noir, instead of settling down to build a highly successful career writing amiably unthreatening humorous pieces for daily newspapers, in which hints of the Decadent world-view and authentically crazed imagination only showed through occasionally.

There are many people in France who still regret that Cros never got credit for inventing the paleophone—although he was far from being the only innovator usurped by the ever-industrious Edison—but lovers of Decadence are entitled to think that it would have been a pity if he had only become famous for the faithful reproduction of other people's endeavors. It would, of course, have been a very different matter if he really had enabled us to communicate with the inhabitants of other worlds by means of light signals, but in that respect too he—like all the rest of us—turned out to be working in a void, lost in a vast deaf-mute universe, overwhelmed by strange regrets.

# XIII.

## The Progress of Literary Satanism

When Jean Des Esseintes recorded the lists of his favorite reading in *À rebours* (1884) he was not really in a position to include anything penned by Anatole-François Thibault, *alias* Anatole France, whose career had hardly got under way at the time. France only published a handful of volumes before 1884, the most notable of which were *Jocasta et le Chat maigre* (1879; tr. as *Jocasta and The Famished Cat*), featuring two disparate novellas, *Le Crime de Sylvestre Bonnard* (1881; *The Crime of Sylvester Bonnard*), a quasi-autobiographical combination of two more novellas about an unworldly booklover's struggle to cope with the vicissitudes of everyday life, and the long moralistic fairy-tale *L'Abeille* (1883; tr. as *Honey-Bee, Bee* and "The Kingdom of the Dwarfs").

The second of these three books had achieved considerable success, but it was brazenly written to please the contemporary reading public, and the author's extensive journalistic enterprises seemed similarly inclined to court popular favor, so his career-track seemed to be developing very differently from the thornier path of which Des Esseintes was far more likely to approve. Even so, Anatole France was eventually to become the principal exponent of one of the central elements of the Decadent world-view: the calculated "literary Satanism" originated by Charles Baudelaire and Gustave Flaubert. The road that led France to that august objective was a strange and winding one, which he pursued with a curiously tortured reluctance, but he evidently felt bound to follow to its bitter end.

Anatole Thibault had had a relatively comfortable youth, ideal for an introverted book-lover because his father—whose nickname, "Père France", he transferred to his pseudonym—owned a prestigious bookshop on the Quai Voltaire. Socially awkward, France much preferred the company of books to that of people, and he was an assiduous scholar, although he was remarkably remiss in the matter of taking examinations and gaining formal qualifications. He was ambitious to write but conspicuously unproductive, and must have seemed something of a good-for-nothing when he refused to take over his father's shop when the latter wanted to retire in 1867; the result of this dereliction of perceived duty was that Père France sold the shop in a fit of pique, and threw his son—who was then twenty-three—out of the family home to fend for himself. Knowing nothing but the book trade, France went to work for Alphonse Lemerre, an ambitious publisher/bookseller with a shop in the Passage Choiseul.

Lemerre's shop hosted the weekly meetings of the Parnassians, a group of poets who considered themselves rebels against Romanticism, although they clung hard to the Gautieresque doctrine of "art for art's sake," and were ambitious to give their work a further degree of independence in that regard. They had published their first showcase anthology, *Le Parnasse contemporain*, in 1866; Baudelaire had contributed a substantial set of *Nouvelles Fleurs du Mal* but died before the Movement could really get under way and remained a phantom presence thereafter. Although the Parnassians' chief activists and propagandists were Catulle Mendès and Louis-Xavier de Ricard, their figurehead was the much older poet Charles Leconte de Lisle, who found the adulation lavished on him by his new disciples very congenial. Initially, France, as a mere shop-assistant, was only allowed to attend Parnassian meetings as a tea-boy, but his wide reading and the articles he contributed to the first issue of Lemerre's new literary periodical, *La Gazette Bibliographique*, in 1868—including a long article on Leconte de Lisle's primary model, Alfred de Vigny—gained him grudging admission to the group, whose other members of a similar age included Paul Verlaine and Stéphane Mallarmé.

The Decadent Movement was eventually to arise in similar fashion to the Parnassians in 1884, when a group of young writers decided that the time had come for yet another new broom to sweep the cobwebs of Romanticism away, but it picked up its initial heroes from the ranks of the Parnassians: Baudelaire became its idol, Verlaine's study of *Poètes maudits* [Accursed Poets] was one of its founding documents, Mendès' journalism provided a key agent of publicity and Mallarmé's symbolist theories were the core of its literary method. One Parnassian left firmly on the sidelines by the advent of calculated Decadence was, however, Anatole France, even though the Belgian writer who wrote under the pseudonym J.-H. Rosny aîné, who was acquainted with all the Decadents but was filed by haphazard circumstance under the Naturalist label, was later to identify France rather than Mallarmé as the true father of Symbolism.

A painfully slow developer in social terms, France gradually gained enough confidence from his attendance at the Parnassian meetings in Lemerre's shop to begin attending *salons* frequented by other members of the group, including one hosted by the art-loving heiress Nina de Callias, who styled her weekly soirée the "*salon des ratés*" [salon of failures] and limited admission—in theory, at least—to writers, painters or composers who had written something too advanced for popular taste. France had already acquired the habit, common among the socially disadvantaged, of becoming infatuated with unattainable women, and he soon became infatuated with Nina. She, for reasons that were not obvious to her other admirers—who considered him ugly as well as *gauche*—seemed to welcome his interest; he helped her compose her contribution to the second anthology of *Le Parnasse contemporain* (1869) and they wrote a one-act play in collaboration, which was rejected by the Comédie Française. Their evolving closeness, however, awoke a jealous rage in Nina's "official" lover, Charles Cros. Cros attacked France physically and nearly succeeded in strangling him before being dragged off. France never attended Nina's *salon* again; when he had worked his way up to serving as co-editor of the third and last Parnassian showcase anthology in 1873—after the inevitable interruption and delay caused by the Franco-Prussian War and the Commune—he blackballed Cros's submissions and continued to abuse him verbally, from a safe distance, for the rest of his life.

Lemerre published the first collection of France's poetry in 1873, but France found poetry difficult and lapsed into the routine production of journalistic articles on literary and bibliographical subjects, especially for *Le Temps*, whose editor was the head of the Bibliothèque du Sénat. After one unsuccessful attempt, France was able to join the staff of that library in 1876, thus securing his future financially. In the meantime he made a new enemy while writing for *Le Temps* by publishing an unkind review of a second edition of Edmond and Jules de Goncourt's *Manette Salomon*, which Edmond intended as a tribute to his recently-deceased younger brother. The grudge thus born kept France isolated thereafter from a significant fraction of the literary society of Paris, for whom Goncourt's *salon*—the "Grenier" [loft]—was its beating heart. Goncourt was a generous man, who did not bar admittance to the Grenier to those who had offended him—Émile Zola often dropped in for the free wine and cigarettes even though the two rival founders of Naturalism loathed one another—but France had a much thinner skin than Zola and stayed away.

Almost as soon as he was secure in his new post as a librarian, the thirty-three-year-old France married Valérie Guérin de Sauville, a twenty-year-old girl from a highly respectable family, who included a court painter among her ancestors. Her substantial dowry enabled them to buy a house. The blissful early years of the marriage coincided with France's first flush of literary success, although he contrived to upset Lemerre by placing his work with Calmann-Lévy, and he also seems to have quarreled with Leconte de Lisle, who was no longer helping his career along. On the other hand, pseudonymous articles written for *L'Univers Illustré*, a weekly periodical issued by Calmann-Lévy, provided laudatory advertisements for several new friends and protégés, including his fellow-Parnassian François Coppée, Alexandre Dumas *fils* and Jules Lemaître, as well as pushing his own work relentlessly.

His success won France welcome admission to several new salons hosted by beautiful and prestigious women, including the Comtesse de Loynes, Madame Aubernon and Madame Arman de Caillavet, all of whom were analogues of Nina de Callias. He took up the opportunities gladly, almost as if he were intent on making up for his earlier disaster. Madame Arman was initially cool towards him, but gradually warmed, eventually issuing a formal invitation in 1886 to him and Valérie to join her for a late-summer holiday in her country house in the Gironde, but clandestinely making it clear that she would be far happier if France came alone. Unhappy with this double-dealing, France did not go at all that year, and when the invitation was repeated the following year he took Valérie with him, thus initiating a keen contest for his affections that Valérie—perhaps surprisingly—was fated to lose.

By the summer of 1888, France was deeply in love with Madame Arman, and in the spring of 1889 he rented a love-nest off the Champs-Élysées where the two of them could meet in secret. Fearful of a scandal, Mme Arman insisted that the affair be kept under wraps, although it could not be hidden from Valérie, who endured four years of it before petitioning for divorce. In the meantime, Madame Arman took a keen interest in France's work, and attempted to involve herself in it. The result of this involvement was a novel that was collaborative in its conception and development, although France took sole charge of the actual writing. Initially entitled *Paphnuce*, the novel was supposed to be a symbolic transfiguration of their love affair.

Based on a legend that France had first transcribed in poetic form as early as 1867, the story that France and Madame Arman elected to develop as a celebration of their love was an obvious by-product of the much better-known legend of the temptation of Saint Anthony. Paphnuce is an eremite living in the Thébaïd, the same north-African region where Anthony endured his famous demonic temptations, and he is similarly afflicted by the Devil's wiles. One of the temptations dangled before him is the memory of an actress named Thaïs, whom he had seen performing erotically-charged roles in Alexandria before his conversion. Convinced that he will have no peace until he defuses the memory by converting the lovely sinner to Christianity, Paphnuce travels to Alexandria in order to find Thaïs and persuade her to repent her wicked ways.

The second part of the narrative offers an account of Thaïs' life-story—including an early baptism and visions of Jesus—and her current luxurious lifestyle, before describing her confrontation with

Paphnuce, who declares his love for her but claims that it is a kind of love that has transcended carnality and is purely spiritual. She laughs at him, but challenges him to accompany her to a banquet of philosophers, at which his stern faith and her desires will both be tested by various Greek-derived sophistications. Like Plato's *Symposium*—on which it is clearly modeled, although it has a very different set of guests—the banquet is an arena in which various theories of love are voiced and supported, but its argument concludes with a demonstrative murder, which horrifies Thaïs and allows Paphnuce to persuade her to abandon her corrupt life of luxury and become a nun—a victory that generates a great deal of hostility among her former admirers, but makes Paphnuce famous in the Christian community.

The final part of the novel, however, describes how Paphnuce's triumph is rendered utterly hollow. Far from being calmed, his obsession is further inflamed. He becomes a stylite and acquires a fine reputation for holiness, but is driven mad by the erotic excitement of which he cannot rid himself, and which his encounter with Thaïs has only served to excite to a further level of intolerability. Eventually, he returns to the nunnery where she had been confined, but finds her dying, already lost to Heaven. His own repentance of his repudiation of carnal love comes too late to win him anything but the angry hostility of the nunnery's superior; the "desperate embrace" in which he seizes Thaïs, in order to "devour her with desire, rage and lust" is a necrophiliac gesture that somehow renders him hideous, and causes the nuns to flee from him in terror, proclaiming that he is a vampire.

It is not entirely clear how Anatole France and Madame Arman contrived to identify with the central characters of this extravaganza, or why they would ever have wanted to, but Madame Arman was apparently delighted with what she considered to be a literary masterpiece. It was she who arranged for its serialization in 1889, as *Thaïs*, in *La Revue des Deux Mondes*, one of the few influential periodicals in which France had so far been unable to publish. The editor, Fernand Brunetière, infuriated France by cutting the text in a seemingly arbitrary fashion, and was promptly added to his hate list.

However absurd it might seem, France really did seem to be able to imagine himself as a Paphnuce reluctantly converted from orthodox asceticism to a finer Epicurean sensibility, in which carnal desire and its indulgence took a central role. When his divorce was finalized in 1893 he and Madame Arman went away together, on a sort of "secret honeymoon" to Florence. While they were there they worked in collaboration, in the same fashion as before, on a new novel—but when they returned, France did not complete the novel immediately, preferring to finish a sequence of loosely-linked short stories that he had begun beforehand, including numerous other ironically reconfigured legends.

The early elements of this series had been collected in *L'Étui de nacre* (1892; tr. as *Tales from a Mother-of-Pearl Casket* and *Mother of Pearl*), which opens with the notorious "Le procurateur de Judea" (tr. as "The Procurator of Judea"), in which an aged Pontius Pilate, reminiscing about old times, reveals that he has no memory whatsoever of his brief encounter with Christ, although he remembers Mary Magdalen very well. The collection also includes a story in which a hermit forms a friendship with a faun and an account of a midnight mass celebrated by souls released from Purgatory. The later stories in the sequence were eventually collected in *Le Puits de Sainte Clare* (1895; tr. as *The Well of Saint Clare*), which took the trends initiated in its predecessor to extremes, especially in three key items: "Saint-Satyr", in which the tomb of an accidentally-canonized satyr becomes the last refuge of all the glory and grandeur of pagan mythology; "Lucifer", in which the handsome fallen angel berates an artist for painting him in hideous guise; and, most strikingly of all, the novella "La Tragédie humaine" (tr. as "The Human Tragedy"), in which a Medieval holy man thrown into prison for criticizing the luxurious lifestyle of rich Churchmen discovers that his only true friend is the liberally-minded Satan, and reluctantly accepts that amity.

By the time that the latter collection was published, France had finished off his second quasi-collaborative celebration of his "conversion", the sentimental love story *Le Lys rouge* (1894; tr. as *The Red Lily*), and published it to considerable acclaim—but the love-affair it transfigured so tenderly was already cooling. The many subsequent trips that France and Madame Arman took together never involved any similar collaboration. From then on, France kept his mistress at arm's length from his writing, and when he moved into a new home in the Villa Saïd early in 1895 he settled into a quasi-eremitic existence, from which Madame Arman was gradually but inexorably excluded. He continued to turn up to her salon, but in the course of the next ten years—during which he became famously embroiled in the Dreyfus affair and underwent a political conversion to communism—he gradually dispensed with her secretarial services, eventually hiring a male secretary in 1904. He eventually split with her completely in 1909, although he handled the parting with remarkable awkwardness, apparently doing everything humanly possible to provoke her to drop him, in order to avoid the embarrassment of having to tell her to her face that it was over.

According to all previous appearances, France was a highly unlikely Dreyfusard and an even more unlikely communist. He had always seemed to be conservative in his views—and, indeed, he continued to seem conservative in his tastes, sticking out like a sore thumb at political meetings of his new allies. He had already been elected to the Académie, so his new affiliations could not spoil his chances, and they probably assisted rather than hindered his eventual award of the Nobel Prize for Literature in 1921, but in Parisian literary society they made him seem a misfit genius, deserving of respect and admiration but direly uncomfortable company.

Although France held his own "open house" once a week at the Villa Saïd, as his magisterial position as the most prestigious writer in France virtually required him to do, people who turned up to it found his habit of not heating the room in the depths of winter severely intimidating, and observed that when he actually condescended to appear, he was always distant and routinely unwelcoming. J.-H. Rosny aîné, who became a regular at Madame Arman's salon—as he was at many others—reported that France spent much of his time there vituperating, not only against people who had personally offended him, or had been offended by him, but against such august predecessors as Victor Hugo and Gustave Flaubert, whose lingering celebrity seemed somehow to detract from his own. Rosny shrewdly remarked that France's animosity toward Flaubert seemed to be born of a determined unwillingness to admit how much *Thaïs* owed, thematically and ideologically, to the example of *La Tentation de Saint-Antoine*.

Having abandoned Madame Arman, long after his infatuation with her had evaporated, and having found new ways to express for his desire for unorthodoxy, it seemed that France had no need to return to the themes that he had developed so extensively in the early days of his life-changing love affair. That flirtation with Decadent style and substance seemed to have been a passing phase, perhaps too idiosyncratic to license any attempt to co-opt him into the burgeoning Decadent Movement—in spite of the manifest wholehearted commitment of *Thaïs* and "La Tragédie humaine" to the Decadent world-view—even if he had not been too towering a figure to be subsumed.

Very few of the works France published between 1895 and 1913 betrayed any conspicuous Decadent sensibility, although *Les Sept femmes de le Barbe-Bleue et autres contes merveilleux* (1909; tr. as *The Seven Wives of Bluebeard and Other Marvellous Tales*) is a collection of ironically perverse fairy-tales, concluding with a long exercise in moral symbolism in which emissaries of an unhappy king search in vein for the shirt of a happy man with which to redeem his melancholy spirit. It was probably motivated by a split between France and the only child of his marriage, his daughter Suzanne, whose controversial second marriage in 1908 he had bitterly opposed. He never spoke to her thereafter, and their estrangement lasted until her death in the 1918 "Spanish flu" epidemic.

As matters transpired, however, France was not yet done with literary Satanism, which he had yet to take to its ultimate extreme. His political conversion gave rise to a number of satirical works, including *Sur la Pierre blanche* (1905; tr. as *The White Stone*) and the famous *L'Île des pingouins* (1906; tr. as *Penguin Island*), but the ultimate satirical product of his eccentric radicalism was the novel that any lover of Decadence must consider to be his literary masterpiece, *La Révolte des anges* (1914; tr. as *The Revolt of the Angels*), which was written on the eve of the outbreak of the Great War.

The story tells how a guardian angel named Arcade is converted to freethought by reading Lucretius' summary of Epicurean philosophy, *De Rerum natura*, in the library of the human he is supposed to be protecting. Leaving his charge to go merrily off the rails of virtue, Arcade sends out a rallying call to the fallen angels, most of whom are working peacefully as teachers and artists, and sets out on a search for Satan, to whom he intends offering the command of an army that will mount a new assault of Heaven. Satan, however, turns out to be a recluse humbly cultivating his garden, who politely declines the offer, on the grounds that liberation from divine tyranny must be won within the hearts and minds of men, not on the field of battle. The force of this undoubtedly-sincere moral did not prevent France from volunteering to bear arms when the war began, but his offer was turned down, presumably politely, on the grounds that he was too old and his genius too precious to be risked in combat.

*La Révolte des Anges* provides a reflective ideological summary of the literary produce of France's infatuation with Madame Arman, deliberately returning to the method of reconfiguring legendary fare with a conscientiously perverse twist. Although many of the earlier stories had been unorthodox love stories, the best of them had dutifully abandoned any trace of carnal passion for something more refined and high-minded, just as France had ultimately succeeded in doing—or, at least, in persuading himself that he had done. Now, instead of identifying himself with a fallen saint wrecked by carnal passion, he identified himself with an angel who jumps rather than falls, and for reasons far more respectably philosophical than the motives that got their claws into Paphnuce. His renegade angel is still an apprentice in the business of rebellion against Divine tyranny, but he follows his Satanic quest to its logical conclusion and obtains his crucial enlightenment directly from the Devil's mouth.

In penning this new transfiguration, France probably fancied that he had freed himself from the last trappings of Decadence, both morally and stylistically, but he was as deluded in that conviction as Paphnuce had been in the conviction that he could save himself by saving Thaïs. There was always more to the Decadent world-view than mere carnal self-indulgence, as Joris-Karl Huysmans could easily have told him, had it not been for the fact that the only salons Huysmans hung out in were ones that France assiduously avoided. As Huysmans demonstrated in his own ostentatious conversion, and Jean Des Esseintes had previously made explicit, carnal indulgences were mere transitory symptoms of a much more deep-seated rebellion against tedious convention, which aimed to reconstruct notions of virtue rather than simply offend them.

Anatole France was not wrong to conclude that the only good friend a virtuous man has in the insistently corrupt world of men is Satan, but he was wrong to imagine that he had found a better way to be Satan's friend than he had in loving Madame Arman rather than his wife. It was, in fact, exactly the same way, although it extrapolated different and less testosterone-fueled instincts. Like it or not—and he could probably have grown to like himself a little better than he did, and much better than he deserved, if he had only tried harder—France really was a thoroughgoing Decadent at heart, even though he was versatile enough to work in different mysterious ways when his moods let him.

# XIV.

## DECADENCE AND THE NOVEL OF THE FUTURE

In two of the key documents that attempted to define and explore the decadent world-view, Charles Baudelaire's "Le Voyage" and "Anywhere Out of the World"—both of which were original inclusions in *Les Fleurs du Mal* (1857)—the sufferer from that world-view, plagued by *ennui* and *spleen*, is imagined as a voyager on a futile quest, searching for something that is nowhere to be found.

In the former item, once the possibilities of the mundane world are exhausted, the weary traveler realizes that the only possibility left to him is that the metaphorical journey actuated by death might constitute a new experience—a possibility that he embraces, ironically, because rather than in spite of his full awareness of its utter futility. The latter item is more direct in its imagination the "voyager" not as a traveler but as a sick man in a hospital, who is only convinced that he would be better off elsewhere because he cannot actually go anywhere at all. (Many of Baudelaire's followers were to undertake actual journeys to "the Orient" in search of a better existential situation, but he had been wise enough to curtail the actual eastward voyage on which his stepfather dispatched him by falling ill, giving himself no option but to return home.) In the second poem the protagonist's mind is pestered by the complaints of his soul, which demands displacement even though it cannot name a destination that will soothe its woe. Its English title was borrowed from Thomas Hood's "The Bridge of Sighs", where the line in question is attributed to a female suicide, thus tacitly reiterating the conviction that death is the final and futile recourse, which souls that can find no resting-place on Earth sometimes rush to meet.

Baudelaire did seek other routes "out of the world", but found them equally unsatisfactory, for reasons explained at length in his assiduous study of the "artificial paradises" of drug-assisted hallucination. His own chosen balm was not death, although there was a certain amount of contributory negligence involved in his dying young, but the creative imagination that actually produced his poems, stories, essays and memoirs. That too was never entirely satisfactory—not least because it always led, inexorably, back to reality and the sordid business of finding outlets for his work—but it did have its compensations. However successful he became in the eye of posterity, though, it was inevitable that Baudelaire seemed a failure to himself—a failure of unparalleled genius, of course, for he was not a modest man, but a failure nevertheless. He could not, in the end, find any destination, even in his art, that satisfied his peevish soul. The particular dimensions of this failure might, however, make it seem a trifle craven to some retrospective observers—all the more so because Baudelaire's restlessness, acute though it was, left more than one avenue unexplored. In retrospect, we can see that one of those avenues was the narrative space of the future.

There might, at first glance, seem to be something paradoxical about the notion of a Decadent image of the future, but there is not. It is, to be sure, an item of Decadent faith that contemporary civilization is on its last legs, having exhausted all its inherent impetus, and that it has no future as an organizational entity but ignominious extinction, but that does not mean that time and history can come to a stop. The whole idea of Decadence emerged from the contemplation of the fate of the Roman Empire, and no such contemplation would have been possible had not European history continued, inexorably, without Rome's tarnished glory, ultimately producing at least one more cultural cycle of the same repetitive sort. Indeed, some historians and Decadent *littérateurs*, on looking back into history, also found it easy to associate the present plight of nineteenth-century France, by analogy, with the declines and falls of Athens, Alexandria, Byzantium, Baghdad, Luxor, Venice, and even, when the mood took them (as it sometimes did) Sodom and Gomorrah.

Clearly, even the most heartfelt subscriber to the Decadent ideology could not imagine that the inevitable decline and fall of European civilization would be a literal end of the world—and could, therefore, legitimately take an interest in what might happen afterwards.

Some Decadent writers did, in fact, dabble in the art of Apocalypse. Critics who see Decadence as one of the darker edges of Romanticism—which is not an unreasonable opinion—are likely to number among its pre-Baudelairean foundation-stones such works as Lord Byron's "Darkness" and the whole sub-genre of Last Man *fantasias* that flourished in the wake of Jean-Baptiste Cousin de Grainville's *Le Dernier homme* (1805). By the same token, the most plangent echoes of Decadent literature to survive the awful progress of the clock of the centuries, which delivered a mortal blow to Decadent sensibility simply by turning 1900, were to be found in such far-futuristic fantasies as J. H. Rosny *aîné*'s "La Mort de la Terre" (1910), William Hope Hodgson's *The Night Land* (1912) and Clark Ashton Smith's tales of Zothique, first published in the 1930s. This observation is, however, only marginally relevant, because apocalypses—however measured and elaborate they might be—are merely the end-point of Baudelaire's "Le Voyage" writ large; they share the same essential sense of futility. They are obviously not a way out of the world but merely another way of bidding it an ironic goodbye.

When Decadent writers went back into the past in their artistic voyages, of course, they were very careful to avoid the strictly historical past and to make what use they could of the marvel-infested mythical past—without, of course, deigning to dabble in the vulgar wish-fulfillments of the conventional marvel tale. The great tradition of lush historical fantasies that made such a robust contribution to the development of the Decadent style—extending from Victor Hugo's *Notre Dame de Paris* (1831) through Théophile Gautier's "Une nuit de Cléopâtre" (1838), Gustave Flaubert's *La tentation de Saint-Antoine* (1874) and Anatole France's *Thaïs* (1890) to Pierre Louÿs' *Aphrodite* (1896)—is very careful to pay more attention to mythical elaboration than to vulgar accuracy in reconstruction, even though it retains a dogged conviction that there is no salvation in miracles. Even when Decadent writers modeled their works on traditional *contes des fées*, after the fashion of Catulle Mendes' classic "Luscignole" (1892), they scrupulously avoided "happy endings", drawing morals from their exercises quite contrary to those approved by the likes of Charles Perrault.

This is not at all surprising, given that the Decadent world-view and sensibility are so intricately bound up with an awareness of historical inexorability; to free the mythical past entirely from the burden of known history, after the fashion of Antoine Galland's *Mille-et-une nuits*, would not have been appropriate. Decadent fantasies tend to be obsessed with the notion of what John Clute called "thinning": the fundamental awareness that the marvelous was always on the wane, doomed to reach exhaustion by virtue of the insistent arrival of the relentlessly mundane and eternally tedious present. This limitation may seem to apply to non-apocalyptic narratives of the future too—which might help to explain why so few Decadent writers attempted them—but there is no logical necessity to determine that tales of the hypothetical young civilization destined to replace the worn-out present should not have the potential to establish artificial paradises without denying the crushing weight of the Juggernaut of history.

There are, in fact, a few Decadent proto-science-fiction stories, most famously the Comte de Villiers de l'Isle Adam's novel *L'Ève future* (1886). Insofar as that novel has a futuristic dimension at all, though, it is trivially apocalyptic. It is also the case that when the unlucky number 1900 killed off the Decadent Movement, many of the Decadent hangers-on who wanted to remain active in the literary arena—including Gustave Le Rouge, Jean de La Hire and Théo Varlet as well as the elder Rosny brother—immediately turned their hands to Wellsian scientific romance, but they too mostly used imminent-future settings and extrapolated their scenarios in tamely apocalyptic directions. Few of them contrived to use future narrative space as a way "out of the world"—as a gateway to the sort of exotica that might have answered the plea of Baudelaire's invalid soul—and none with any conspicuous artistic success. It is not obvious why that should be the case, and why are there so few Decadent novels of the future, even by post-Decadent science fiction writers, that are anything more than celebrations of doom on a larger scale than the individual.

Oblique assistance in providing an answer of sorts is offered by Félix Bodin's *Le Roman de l'avenir* (1834; tr. as *The Novel of the Future*), which was written specifically to stake a claim to the idea of writing a novel (as opposed to an apocalypse or a utopia) set in the future. The book aspires to present the first exemplary specimen of a new genre—*le roman futuriste* [futuristic novel]—and features an elaborate commentary, in the form of a preface, an introduction, a postscript and notes, on the potential difficulties and rewards of such a project. Bodin, who was then a serving *député* in the parliament that had taken control of France following the July Revolution 1830, described the hurried project as a "hoax", borrowing the word from English and defining it as something "seriously farcical and farcically serious"; one element of this calculated ambiguity is its title, which refers not only to the possibility of using the future as a narrative space in a novel, but also to the potential future of the novel as an art-form. This was a topic that Bodin considered interesting, because he felt that there was something essentially absurd, and something essentially unhealthy, about the affectations of the popular Romantic novels of his own day.

Writing in 1834, Bodin considered the presiding genius of French Romanticism to be Jean-Jacques Rousseau, by virtue of the still-thriving cult of *sensibilité* that Rousseau had launched, and he deemed Charles Nodier, rather than the up-and-coming Victor Hugo, to be the movement's contemporary figurehead. Like Jane Austen, Bodin favored polite common sense over Rousseauesque sensibility, and like Jane Austen, he thought that the flood of Gothic novels (*romans noir* in French) that had been the most conspicuous literary phenomenon of the last decade of the eighteenth century and the first decade of the nineteenth had been not merely ludicrous but potentially injurious to young and impressionable minds. For Bodin, "Romantic" implied "Gothic", and "absurdly over-melodramatic", so the whole Romantic philosophy—in its upbeat as well as its downbeat manifestations—seemed to him to be opposed to the further progress of democracy and capitalism, of which he was strongly in favor, and locked in opposition to the concept and value that he held higher than any other: *civilization*.

The French word *civilization* implies rather more than its English equivalent; it was routinely used to refer to the process of educating children as well as the business of living in cities, and literature had long been regarded as a potentially useful instrument of moral education. It is hardly surprising, given this emphatic double meaning, that French ethnographers inspired by the great exploratory voyages of the eighteenth century were in the forefront of a theoretical tendency to draw analogies between "the savage mind"—i.e., the thought-processes of preliterate tribesmen—and the unformed minds of children. Nor is it surprising that Jean-Jacques Rousseau, the champion of "noble savagery", should recommend in his own treatise on education, *Émile* (1762), that children should not be given books to read at all (with the single exception of *Robinson Crusoe*) lest they be corrupted by civilization. Félix Bodin, by contrast, was a great believer in civilization, in both senses of the word; its progress was, in his view, the true goal of politics and literature alike—and he believed that, while contemporary politics often threw up frustrating obstacles to that progress, contemporary literature was, in the main, undermining it.

This is, to some extent, an odd judgment. It was generally believed at the time (and still is, to some extent) that art and civilization went hand-in-hand, and that works of art—including works of literature—were among the best indicators of a civilization's attainments. Bodin believed, in fact, that this had been true almost throughout history—but that the association had recently broken down. Since the Revolution of 1789, he thought, the further progress of civilization had been busy eclipsing "the poetry of the past", because science and common sense had leached all the plausibility out of traditional ideas of "the marvelous". He saw Romanticism as a sort of last-ditch defense of "the poetry of the past", ludicrously exaggerated by its own desperation into something as absurd as it was unhealthy—but he was optimistic that the future might produce a new "poetry of civilization", complete with its own technological version of "the marvelous". Fortunately or unfortunately, it was not to be so easy, as his own tentative experiment readily proved.

Romantic literature, in Bodin's eyes, was not merely a threat to civilization because of its nostalgic regard for the past, embracing a fascination with Medieval codes of behavior and Medieval superstition, but also because of its glorification of Rousseau's *sensibilité*: the spontaneity of emotion conceived as an instinctive source of virtue. In the future, Bodin thought—or, at least, hoped—both these fascinations would be reversed; the novel of the future would be fascinated by the future, and the possibilities of further social and technological progress, and a key element of that progress would be the substitution of sense for sensibility, a celebration of the triumph of the intellect over the emotions.

We now know, of course, that this was not what actually happened. Bodin would doubtless have been disappointed to learn that the aspects of Romanticism that he considered morbid would be pushed to their extreme in Decadent literature, but he would have been even more disappointed had he anticipated the actual state of late twentieth-century literature, and the extent to which it still championed sensibility over sense, emotion over science, and nostalgia over civilization.

Bodin complained in his preface to *Le Roman de l'avenir* that previous literary attempts to use the future as a narrative space had done no more than paint utopian hopes and apocalyptic anxieties, but the attempts he made to import an exploratory spirit into his own "futuristic novel" failed, bogged down as they were in the quagmire of his own hopes and anxieties. The late twentieth century that he imagined was, in large measure, the fulfillment of the various programs that he tried to advanced in his parliamentary career and the culmination of his particular ideals of social and technological progress, and what dramatic tension his story had was derived entirely from the nagging nightmare that afflicted those hopes: the possibility of a violent resurgence of everything that moral progress ought to render obsolete.

The fragment of a story constructed to exemplify *Le Roman de l'avenir* was, in spite of the author's best intentions, a tale of runaway sensibility: of love gone wrong, and counter-revolution unconfined. The world described therein is democratically ordered and politically well-administered, but there is a vast conspiracy against it, whose core unites three principal parties: the relics of the old aristocracy, the relics of the old military establishment and the relics of the old Church. Significantly, this conspiracy calls itself the Poetic, or Universal Anti-Prosaic, Association, its ranks also being swelled by a legion of writers and artists. Romanticism is not only alive and kicking in Bodin's late twentieth century, but still has a monopoly on the glamour and dash that even Bodin cannot, in all honesty, credit to dutiful writers loyal to the cause of civilization and the intellect. In this, at least, Bodin was a true prophet—and it is perhaps for this reason, however paradoxical it might seem, that future narrative space could not accommodate the paradisal oasis for which the writers who embraced the Decadent world-view claimed to be in search, or anything else authentically "out of the world". It was not only Bodin's "novel of the future" that could not escape the straitjacket that made it very much a novel of the present, but *any* "novel of the future".

Literary Decadence was, to some extent, a reaction against the myth of progress that Bodin held so dear. Decadent philosophy was by no means averse to technology; indeed, it glorified the artificial, valuing it far more highly than the natural, and was therefore wholeheartedly in favor of anything that would make artifice cleverer. Decadent philosophy flatly refused to believe, however, that there was any necessary connection between technological advancement and social progress, and did not think this lack of connection in the least unfortunate. Decadent philosophy was not Rousseauesque, in the sense that it thought that there was something essentially virtuous about *sensibilité*, but it did put a high priority on sensual indulgence, and was therefore antipathetic to the moral aspects of educational civilization. Items that Bodin bundled together, therefore—because he thought them causally, if not intrinsically, linked—were conspicuously disaggregated within the Decadent world-view. Within the Decadent world-view, the instrumental aspects of civilization—the artifices of city life—are, or ought to be, quite separate from the process of civilizing children, or adults, with patiently stern lessons in good behavior.

Given all this, a writer embracing the Decadent world-view would not have been at all surprised that Bodin's ham-fisted attempt to construct a novel of the future had gone so awkwardly awry, and might well have been able to form a more accurate judgment of the futility of their making any attempt of the same sort. Subscribers to the Decadent Movement knew perfectly well—and, indeed, frequently boasted—that their works were antipathetic to the intellectual thrust of nineteenth-century civilization. Far from hoping, as Bodin did, that their society might make further social and moral progress, they were—by definition—convinced that it was on its last legs, tottering towards collapse and ruination. Unlike the rebels of Bodin's hypothetical twentieth century, however, they did not believe that their own kind of "poetry" might be renewed and revitalized by some kind of revolution against the cerebral "poetry of civilization"; they accepted that it was as redundant as any other aspect of civilization in decay, and would share in its collapse. Although it was inherent in their world-view that time would not stop when that collapse occurred—that there would be a post-apocalyptic narrative space in which novels of the future might be set—it was also inherent in their world-view that the novels of that future would not embrace the poetry of Decadence, nor the broader poetry of Romanticism, even if the hypothetical poetry of what Bodin considered to be civilization never came to pass. Whether or not future civilization would have a poetry of its own, they assumed, it was inaccessible to their own—which was, indeed, firmly tied to the mythical and historical past by its language and its patterns of symbolism.

Twentieth-century futuristic fiction has, of course, included many bold attempts to imagine completely different futures, but it is not obvious that any of them have avoided the trap that Bodin set for himself and duly fell into. Even if we discount the vast majority that merely tried to dress up the past's stereotyped images of the marvelous in new pseudoscientific disguises, we can easily see—as Bodin could not—that the imagined marvels of civilization and technology have not lived up to his optimistic hopes. Although there is a fugitive enclave of the mythical future that is better than stupid transfigurations of that past-that-never-was, it has only achieved that status by transfiguring the people it represents as characters, liberating them from the burdens of the mythical past—including the burdens of *sensibilité*. Bodin imagined that as a good thing, while thinking hypothetically, but he was all too well aware that many people would not agree with him; not only is his own fragment of a futuristic novel shot through with sarcastic laments that readers—especially female readers—will not like it (because it is not Romantic enough) but it is also saturated with an awareness of its own failure (because it is still too Romantic). Modern futurist fiction has not escaped that dilemma; to the extent that it is authentic, most contemporary readers hate it, because it is not Romantic enough, while it still fails to meet its own objectives because it is still too Romantic.

Decadent futurists, in the nineteenth and the twentieth centuries, would have been no more able to avoid this trap than true believers in progress. Unlike most of the would-be futurists who have attempted to use the relevant narrative space constructively, though, they would have been well aware of their inability to escape the present, to find a way "out of the world" that was more than tawdry illusion. They would have known that images of future civilizations in their own decadence could only be pointless transfigurations of the present, while images of future civilizations that had not yet reached their own decadent phase could only lapse into absurd transfigurations of the past. They would have known, too, what Bodin glimpsed and Anatole France once specifically stated: that any present-day writer who actually contrived to foresee the artifice of the future, together with its actual moral order, would alienate present-day readers by virtue of his success.

Only present-day writers who viewed the future instrumentality of civilization through the lenses of contemporary moral education could expect a sympathetic response from readers; since Decadent methodology involved a flat refusal to view the present instrumentality of civilization through the lenses of contemporary moral education, no Decadent writer was about to make that compromise. Future narrative space did not, in fact, offer a way "out of the world" at all, but only a more tortuous way back into it, and not the most edifying one, no matter how much exotic scenery could be mustered as *décor*.

It would not be true to say that those would-be Decadents who eventually threw in the towel, and became writers of scientific romance instead, shed their Decadent world-views like a snake sloughing its skin. They mostly maintained the assumption that the world was still going from bad to worse, and that the march of technological artifice could not possibly ameliorate that deterioration, even if it did not actually make it worse. They did, however—without exception—compromise with the expectations of their readers by leavening the essential darkness of their Romanticism with a few optimistic gestures. They did not always contrive "happy endings", and often did what they could to make it obvious that they did not believe in any such ending, hating the necessity of invoking whatever hollow *deus ex machina* convention had forced them to provide, but for the most part, they simply refused to take what they were doing seriously, writing rapidly and in a deliberately slapdash fashion; in that respect, many subsequent writers of science fiction followed their example. The most conspicuous feature of twentieth-century quasi-Decadent futurism is its deliberate crudity, its tacit denial of its own possibility. This does not mean that its prose is necessarily unstylish—sometimes it is very stylish indeed—but it does mean that it is always mocking, with respect to its authorial ambition as well as its anticipated audience response.

At the end of the day, one of the fundamental assumptions of the Decadent world-view is that, even though it is the only thing that any sane person could sensibly want, it is quite impossible to get "out of the world". Like sex, death, music and drugs, future narrative space is an illusory exit; it cannot lead to paradise—"paradise" in this sense, meaning a state of being devoid of ennui, spleen and impuissance—or even to a satisfactory playground. This is not altogether bad news, however, because another fundamental assumption of the Decadent world-view is that heroic attempts to get "out of the world", if they are rationally directed, can take one further *in*, towards the nitty-gritty of both emotional experience and its intellectual obligation. Like the conventional literature of hesitation and suspense, which deals with the strategic delay of such consummations as sex and death, future narrative space does have some potential as an idiosyncratic form of artifice, as an instrument of enlightenment as well as an instrument of distraction. It is a potential that has, as yet, only been explored in relatively crude ways, but it is still there—and it really is the case that time and history will not stop, even when we have administered the ecocatastrophic *coup-de-grâce* to the process of cultural self-destruction that the Decadent writers of the nineteenth century anticipated and the Great War dutifully began

# XV.

## EDGAR POE AND THE GOTHIC LIFESTYLE

Mick Mercer states in his survey of *The Hex Files: The Goth Bible* (1896) that "from the point of view of the future Goth cult, Poe is crucial", and that "Poe sets out, in the introduction to 'The Murders in the Rue Morgue', a perfect description of how a literate Goth....might express his fantasy". The passage in question describes how the relatively well-off narrator discovers a kindred spirit in the eccentric Auguste Dupin and is permitted "the expense of renting, and furnishing in a style which suited the rather fantastic gloom of our common temper, a time-eaten and grotesque mansion, long deserted through superstitions into which we did not inquire, and tottering to its fall in a retired and desolate portion of the Faubourg St Germain". There the two men live a secluded life, admitting no visitors and going out only by night. The narrator observes:

> "It was a freak of fancy in my friend to be enamored of the night for her own sake; and into this bizarrerie, as into all his others, I quietly fell; giving myself up to his wild whims with a perfect abandon. The sable divinity would not herself dwell with us always; but we could counterfeit her presence. At first dawn of the morning we closed all the massy shutters of our old building; lighted a couple of tapers which, strongly perfumed, threw out only the ghastliest and feeblest of rays. By the aid of these we then busied our souls in dreams—reading, writing or con-

versing until warned by the clock of the advent of the true Darkness."

There can be little doubt that Poe considered Dupin to be a fantastic projection of himself; the third Dupin story, "The Mystery of Marie Roget", details a process of ratiocination which he developed himself in respect of an actual case. In real life, of course, Poe found no benefactor willing to rent a crumbling mansion where he might live in the manner described, and perhaps he would not really have liked to. There is certainly an element of parodic humor in his description, but that playfulness merely serves to mask the self-indulgent sincerity of his fantasy. It is certainly the case that some few of his readers found something deeply appealing in the notion: something which touched their own calculated perversity and private self-indulgence. Indeed, Mick Mercer's comments demonstrate that the passage is still capable of striking a chord today.

Among the American writers who carried forward the tradition of weird fiction which Poe instituted only one made much of an effort to live according to the ideal sardonically described in "The Murders in the Rue Morgue": H. P. Lovecraft, who died in 1937. This is testimony to the fact that Poe's character and literary methods were developed in frank and extreme opposition to the general tenor of American values and American culture, but the tenacious influence which Lovecraft has had over a small but vociferous minority of American writers is clear proof of the fact that others shared his particular species of opposition. Lovecraft made very little money when he was alive and did not live to see a single volume of his works published, but he became and has remained the central figure of a highly distinctive form of horror fiction, best exemplified by his tales of what his friend and posthumous publisher, August Derleth, dubbed "the Cthulhu Mythos".

Poe's influence outside his native land was, on the other hand, very considerable indeed, being most marked in the city in which he was careful to set the home of Auguste Dupin: Paris. Poe's French translator was Charles Baudelaire, whom Théophile Gautier identified as the great pioneer and paradigm example of the "Decadent style". According to Gautier, Decadent style is "ingenious, complicated, clever, full of delicate hints and refinements, gathering all the delicacies of speech, borrowing from technical vocabularies, taking color from every palette, tones from all musical instruments, contours vague and fleeting, listening to translate subtle confidences, confessions of depraved passions and the odd hallucinations of a fixed idea turning to madness". Such a style is, Gautier states, "summoned to express all and to venture to the very extremes", and he quotes with approval Baudelaire's own stated fascination with "the phosphorescence of putrescence".

Like Poe, Baudelaire had a stepfather who, though relatively wealthy, refused to support his literary career (in Baudelaire's case the crime was compounded by the fact that his legitimate inheritance was being withheld on the grounds that he was allegedly not fit to manage his own affairs). Like Poe, Baudelaire felt that his mother had remarried beneath her and that he was nobler than his stepfather by reason of blood and temperament alike. Like Poe, Baudelaire lived perennially beyond his means, seeking solace in escapist dreams which he made into an art form. It is hardly surprising that he thought himself a kindred spirit, and took Poe's lessons to heart.

Under the influence of the aesthetic theories of George "Beau" Brummell (who was, like Poe, taken far more seriously in France than in his native England) Baudelaire adopted a style of dress in which black was predominant, and he dedicated himself to the business of being a soul in torment, unleashing the full heroic fervor of his imagination against the draconian threats of *ennui* (morbid tedium) and *spleen* (acrimonious depression). His amplification of Poe's literary and intellectual affectations redoubled their power and influence.

It is not in the famous poems collected in *Les Fleurs du Mal* (1857) that Baudelaire's lifestyle fantasies achieve their most poignant expression, but rather in the poems in prose that he intended to gather together under the title *Spleen de Paris* (he died before completing the project). These include such lyrical hymns to escapism as "Anywhere out of the World" (1857), whose title—in English in the original—is derived from Thomas Hood's morbid poem about suicide "The Bridge of Sighs", and "L'Invitation au voyage" (1862). The most revealing of them all, perhaps, is "La Chambre double"

(1862), in which the poet imagines himself in a wonderful room where "the soul bathes in idleness, amid the aromas of regret and desire", where "the furniture too seems to be dreaming" and "the fabrics speak a language of silence", inhabited by an invisible Goddess whose "eyes....burn bright in the twilight; subtle and terrifying mirrors of the soul, whose fearful malice I know so well". Alas, no sooner has the poet declared that "Time is banished; it is Eternity which rules this place: an Eternity of delights!" than he is recalled to reality by a knocking on the door and he sees his room as it actually is: a "tawdry place of infinite tedium" where "the rankness of desolation lies upon everything" and the only object that can bring a smile to his face is a vial of laudanum. Time's empire is restored and the burden of mundanity reimposed: "Sweat, slave! Live, and be damned!"

A generation after his death, Baudelaire became the parent of the Decadent Movement launched by Paul Verlaine's 1884 anthology of the works of *Poètes maudits* [Accursed Poets], which also included samples from the long-vanished but not-yet-dead Arthur Rimbaud. The lifestyle defined by Dupin and refined by Baudelaire was further elaborated by several of the Decadent writers, and the central prose document of the movement, Joris-Karl Huysmans' *À rebours* (1884, usually translated as *Against the Grain*, although the most faithful translation, puiblished by Penguin, is titled *Against Nature*) may be regarded as an extraordinary elaboration of it.

The hero of *À rebours*, Jean Des Esseintes, has already abandoned all the activities traditionally associated with active Decadence, having concluded his experimentation with sex and drugs. He has secluded himself in a house in an unfashionable district of Paris in order that he may restrict his intercourse with other human beings to the appreciation of their works of art—which is, he asserts, the only kind of human contact worth having. With the aid of modern artifice, he decides, he can reproduce in the comfort of his own home any experience worth having; for instance, all that is worthwhile about a sea voyage can be synthesized with the aid of suitable dress, fishing-tackle, a few sound-effects, a briny odor and a copy of Poe's *Narrative of Arthur Gordon Pym*.

Des Esseintes' opinions as to which works of art are worth keeping are calculatedly heretical (praising Baudelaire's prose-poetry above all else), as are his comments on morality, which casually overturn all the commonly-accepted precepts of his day. His greatest triumph of inversion comes, however, when he mistakenly assumes that a doctor's prescription for a strength-building diet is a prescription for an enema and begins taking his daily nourishment via the wrong end of the alimentary canal. His final decision to embrace the Catholic Church is not a repentance; he commits himself precisely because he knows that belief in God is absurd and that faith is the ultimate fantasy.

À rebours is, of course, an extended joke (although some of its readers contrive not to notice its hilarity) but part of the novel's charm is that its playful fantasies are authentically appealing, at least to that alienated minority of human beings whose tastes and opinions run contrary both to those of the majority and those of the majority-sanctioned cultural élite. Huysmans wrote the book while working as a clerk for the French equivalent of the Home Office, and generations of critics have taken delight in telling readers that his description of des Esseintes' lifestyle is partly based and what Stéphane Mallarmé was able to tell him about the apartments of the celebrated man-about-town Comte Robert de Montesquiou. In fact, Huysmans needed little inspiration from that quarter; he had, after all, read Poe and Baudelaire and had fantasies enough of his own. He also had the opportunity to observe other Decadent affectations in the cafés and salons.

Huysmans was a close friend of the journalist Jean Lorrain, who nurtured a poisonous envious hatred for Montesquiou because the Comte was everything that he aspired (hopelessly) to be: a hereditary aristocrat whose flamboyant homosexuality was condoned by high society and upon whom the actress Sarah Bernhardt—the superstar of fashionable Paris—positively doted. It was not until 1887 that Lorrain became rich enough to furnish a house in the Rue de Courty according to his tastes, but he must have discussed his ambitions with Huysmans when they first became friends in 1883, and doubtless relayed rumors he had heard in the small Normandy village where he was born of the fabulous décor favored by the neighborhood's most notorious English exile, Algernon Swinburne, which he was later to imitate. Lorrain took ether—a drug far more powerful and dangerous than the laudanum that Baudelaire favored or the hashish he was reluctant to try—and he wrote numerous tales of horrific hallucination set in his own "haunted house". His novel *Monsieur de Phocas* (1901; English translation 1994) provided a suitably phantasmagorical account of his own version of the Decadent personality and lifestyle.

Another of Huysmans' close acquaintances was Berthe Courrière, sometime mistress of Remy de Gourmont and acolyte of the would-be Rosicrucian magus Joséphin Péladan. Péladan was by far the most spectacular of the lifestyle fantasists of *fin-de-siècle* Paris, building on the example of the self-styled Éliphas Lévi much as the members of the English Order of the Golden Dawn did; he and other people to whom Courrière introduced Huysmans cropped up, lightly disguised, in Huysmans' quasi-documentary novel about fashionable Satanism, *Là-Bas* (1891). Some of their adventures were undertaken in the company of Villiers de l'Isle Adam, an impoverished aristocrat whose bitterness at not being able to repair his fortunes is amply displayed by his classic collection of *Contes cruels* (1883)—another work highly praised by Des Esseintes in *À rebours*—which gave its name to a whole new subgenre of fiction. Remy de Gourmont went on to become the critical mainstay of the Decadent Movement, having been forced into seclusion after his features were destroyed by the disfiguring disease *lupus erythrematosus*.

The repercussions of Huysmans' thought-experiment in lifestyle fantasy were, of course, widespread. Huysmans was not present when Jean Lorrain persuaded Marcel Schwob to bring Oscar Wilde to dine at the haunted house (Anatole France, who was to bring French literary Satanism to its magnificent climax in *The Revolt of the Angels* in 1914, completed the party of four) but Wilde was a great admirer of *À rebours*, and paid due homage to it in *The Picture of Dorian Gray*, where it appears as the "yellow book" that inspires Dorian to make the most of his unprecedented opportunity to live his life as an incorruptible work of art.

The English Decadent Movement was, of course, a pale shadow of its French parent. It labored under the handicap of Victorian standards of decency and it was conclusively slain by the condemnation of Wilde to two years hard labor and universal ignominy; its supporters instantly relabeled themselves Symbolists, having learned from Mallarmé that that was the safest route to near-respectability. During the two or three years that it flourished, however, the English Decadent Movement did produce one marvelously extravagant lifestyle fantasist in Count Stanislaus Eric Stenbock, author of the stridently homoerotic *Studies in Death* (1893)—who reportedly delighted in boasting that he slept in a coffin and shared his dinner-table with a pet toad—and one equally extravagant homage to Poe's Auguste Dupin in M. P. Shiel's *Prince Zaleski* (1895).

Dupin's most famous English descendant is, of course, Sherlock Holmes, whose lifestyle, as described in *A Study in Scarlet* (1887), had a few marked Decadent touches. Under the influence of the terminally tedious Dr. Watson and the pressure of fame, however, Holmes became a rather less flamboyant character whose nocturnal habits and drug-addiction were gradually de-emphasized. No such domestication spoiled Zaleski, who easily outdid all his rivals in status and style. His own recorder describes his home as "a vast tomb of Mausoleums in which lay deep sepulchres how much genius, culture, brilliancy, power!"

In Zaleski's room the narrator observes that: "Even in the semi-darkness of the very faint greenish lustre radiated from an open censerlike lampas of fretted gold in the centre of the domed encausted roof, a certain incongruity of barbaric gorgeousness in the furnishing filled me with amazement. The air was heavy with the scented odour of this light, and the fumes of the narcotic cannabis sativa."

Holmes, of course, favored the musical distraction of the violin, but Zaleski is otherwise inclined. "One side of the room," reports the chronicler of his exploits, "was occupied by an organ whose thunder in that circumscribed place must have set all these relics of dead epochs clashing and jingling in fantastic dances."

This is as good a point as any at which to break off the elaborate cataloguing of Poe's influence in order to comment the close affinities between the lifestyle fantasies of the Decadents of the 1880s and some lifestyle fantasies of more recent provenance—affinities that drew Mick Mercer to make his inspired observation regarding the crucial significance of Poe to the ideals and affectations of contemporary Goths.

The essence of the modern Gothic lifestyle is, of course, its twofold opposition. Born of the punk backlash against excessively-commercialized and increasingly bombastic popular music, it began as a rejection of both the values of the cultural élite and the values of the orthodox majority. It symbolized this double rejection by a series of emblematic oppositions broadly similar to those adopted by Poe's Decadent disciples: black dress and a mock-morbid outlook on life; a declared preference for night over day and pallor over suntan; a fondness for images of death (and, with cunning propriety, undeath) and baroque forms of personal decoration; a sometimes-hesitant sympathy towards sexual fetishism; etc, etc.

Given this fundamental similarity of outlook and affectation it is entirely natural that active Goths have made considerable progress in plundering the same cultural heritage as the Decadents. It is significant that although Mick Mercer refuses to make room in his Gothic canon for the Damned ("Image is not a qualification") or the Cure ("always were and always will be a pop band") he does make room for the avantgardist exploits of Diamanda Galas, whose works include a musical rendition of Baudelaire's pioneering exercise in explicit literary Satanism "Les Litanies de Satan" (from *Les Fleurs du mal*). Given this, there is no surprise in the fact that the history of the embryonic genre records that the calculated but rather content-free heresies of Christian Death have given way to the more carefully elaborated paganism of Fields of the Nephilim and Incubus Succubus, which bands like the Garden of Delight and Endura have eclectically allied with imagery borrowed from quasi-Rosicrucian symbolic magic and H. P. Lovecraft.

All this imagistic apparatus is as serviceable now as it was a hundred years ago—which is only to be expected, given that its primary appeal then was its flagrant anachronism. It is worth remembering that the word "Gothic" first acquired its modern meaning as a sneering dismissal of elements in architecture—and later of literature—that were considered "primitive" and "barbarous" by the Classically-minded. It is worth remembering, too, that it is wholly in keeping with the Gothic outlook that a sneer should be adopted as a banner to be worn with resentful pride.

There is an appealing incongruity in the fact that both Auguste Dupin and Prince Zaleski were detectives. Had they not prostituted themselves thus, they would probably never have got into print, but their crime-solving was really no more than a convenient way to demonstrate their mental superiority. They were not as other men, because they could see through the hollow sham of genteel appearances to the malevolence and perversity which lay beneath, ever ready to erupt in enigmatic deviance. They operated in the days before the fledgling institution that employed Joris-Karl Huysmans had spawned the methodical scientific processes of detection that nowadays makes detective work routine, but even then it was obvious that they had no business trifling with trivia; their subject-matter was not so much the criminal as the bizarre, and of that they were true connoisseurs. It is in that respect that modern Goths might legitimately seek to emulate them—and, of course, to savor the kind of thunder in circumscribed place which "set all these relics of dead epochs clashing and jingling in fantastic dances."

# XVI.

## FASHIONS IN FAITHFULNESS:
## THE DECADENCE OF ERNEST DOWSON

In the 1964 study of the work of Ernest Dowson that he wrote for Twayne's "English Authors" series, Thomas Burnett Swann—who vies with Clark Ashton Smith for the right to be considered the last of the great Decadent fantasists—is admirably forthright in refusing to consider his subject as a mere Aesthete rather than a wholehearted Decadent. Swann begins his essay with the observation that the term Decadent is "much more descriptive of [Dowson's] art, with its air of decay and finality and its morbid concern with death."

Hindsight assures us that the morbid concern in question was desperately relevant. Dowson died at the age of thirty-three in the final year of the nineteenth century, six months before Oscar Wilde and six years after the double suicide of his parents. He was slain by tuberculosis, which he had deliberately complicated with alcoholism and wormwood poisoning. His once-close friendship with Wilde had disintegrated, killed by absurdity: Wilde, busy dying beyond his means, was bitterly resentful of poor Dowson's inability to repay a small loan.

Hindsight should also inform us, however, that Dowson's morbidity developed far in advance of his personal distress. His life and career after leaving Oxford in 1888—without a degree—raced downhill like a runaway cart, gathering velocity all the while. It remains unclear, even to this day, why this should have been the case, and we will never know for sure. In order to arrive at a final answer we would have to strip away all the layers of confusion with which the poet carefully surrounded himself. All such work is guesswork, and even if one were to guess the truth, it would be incapable of proof. For this uncertainty any true Decadent ought, of course, to be properly grateful.

The conventional account of Dowson's poetry, offered up by the poet himself and conscientiously reiterated by his critics, is that the bulk of it—most especially "Cynara", the poem on which his enduring fame is most solidly based—was inspired by his love for Adelaide Foltinowicz, the twelve-year-old daughter of a Polish restaurateur. Dowson became fixated upon her in 1891, the year in which he published what he initially entitled "Non sum qualis eram bonae sub regno Cynarae" (it is mainly for the convenience of critics that it is nowadays known merely as "Cynara").

None of Dowson's friends could understand his declared obsession. Frank Harris was one of several who insisted that Adelaide was not merely unworthy of his adoration but not even pretty. The aspersions that they cast in the hope of breaking his apparent addiction continued to be cast after his death; Swann dutifully repeats the rumor that Adelaide went completely to the bad and died a syphilitic whore, although he declines to support the allegation that she provided the inspiration for Somerset Maugham's novel *Of Human Bondage*.

Dowson brushed off such complaints with the blithe assurance that if they could only see Adelaide through his eyes, they would understand. None of the complainers seems to have doubted his sincerity; the fact that he was acting out the central fantasy of his first short story, "Souvenirs of an Egotist" (1888)—in which a classical violinist remains self-deceptively obsessed with a pre-puberal female organ-grinder he once met in earliest youth—was merely taken as confirmation of the fact that he shared the same innocently paedophilic inclinations as Lewis Carroll and John Ruskin. The fact that the motif was repeated in most of his other prose works was taken as additional proof of the general fascination that somehow—and rather arbitrarily—became narrowly focused on Adelaide.

Dowson's friends and critics were and remain unanimous in their blithe acceptance of the claim that the deep disappointment occasioned by the fact that Adelaide, at fourteen, refused to marry him, and ultimately broke his heart when she married her father's waiter three years later. Why should they doubt him, given that he was so busily engaged in the work of patient self-destruction, employing the weapon whose fatality and futility he described with such loving care in his prose poem "Absinthia Taetra"? On the other hand, why should they have taken him entirely seriously, given that he manifested the customary Decadent fascination with masks and impostures?

Dowson, who made his living—insofar as he made it at all—by translating novels from the French, was very well aware of the fascination that the French Decadents had for masques and theatrical make-up. The first of the two collaborative novels he wrote with Arthur Moore—which attempted to reproduce Henry James's sly prurience as well as his realistic manner—was entitled *A Comedy of Masks*, and his most substantial poem was the verse drama "The Pierrot of the Minute".

The whole point of donning a mask is, of course, to cloak one's true identity, and if the job is well enough done the truth becomes irrecoverable. It is conceivable that Dowson was no better than anyone else at penetrating the literary masks paraded by other writers, but it seems improbable. He was surely better placed than anyone else to understand what his principal literary idol, Algernon Swinburne, had done in *Atalanta in Calydon*, in which the character of Atalanta is almost certainly a mask designed to disguise from puritan readers the fact that the poem's true object of fascination is not really female at all (why else would Meleager's mother complain that his pursuit of "strange loves" will be the death of her, and why else would Plexippus call Meleager a "man grown girl" and "woman-tongued" because he is attracted to Atalanta?)

There is, of course, no way that anyone will ever know for sure to whom "Cynara" is actually addressed, and some might think that there is no obvious reason to doubt Dowson's insistence that it was addressed to a twelve-year-old waitress whose charms were invisible to everyone but him, but it is surely worth considering other theses, if only because that might allow us to understand what the poem's celebrated refrain might actually mean.

The original title of "Cynara" is taken from an ode by the Latin poet Horatius Flaccus, better known as Horace. Swann translates it as "I am not what once I was in kind Cynara's day". No one has the faintest idea who Horace's Cynara might have been, and that is presumably why Dowson employed the name. We do, however, know exactly how and where he composed his own poem: he scribbled it on whatever materials came readily to hand in a disreputable alehouse called the Cock.

The first verse of Dowson's poem laments that "yesternight, betwixt her lips and mine/There fell thy shadow, Cynara! thy breath was shed/Upon my soul between the kisses and the wine;/And I was desolate and sick of an old passion". The second verse relates how the poet's continued congress with the female in question, despite the fact that "the kisses of her bought red mouth were sweet", is haunted and diminished by the sickness of that same "old passion". The third verse regrets that much of that old passion has been half-forgotten—"gone with the wind"—while the fourth recounts that the poet "cried for madder music and for stronger wine" in a desperate but futile account to retain and confirm that forgetfulness. After confirming yet again that "I am desolate and sick of an old passion" the last verse ends, as all its predecessors have, with the ringing declaration that "I have been faithful to thee, Cynara! in my fashion".

"I have been faithful to thee in my fashion" has survived sterling service as a Decadent catch-phrase to become an authentic cliché, parroted and recognized even today by many who know nothing of its origin and have never heard of Dowson. It is conceivable, however, that its current users—who are content to revel luxuriously in the formula's ironic hypocrisy—understand it a little better than those critics who seem happy enough to accept that the poem's Cynara is Adelaide Foltinowicz. Swann admits, of course, that Adelaide could not have qualified as an "old passion", but takes a familiar line in arguing that the poet's inspiration must therefore have been "an ideal of innocence which he soon came to identify with her". His consequent deduction that the "pale, lost lilies" of the third verse "symbolize the innocence of Cynara" is typical of this mode of decoding.

This interpretation is forced to hold that the guilty sentiment confessed and simultaneously denied by the phrase "faithful...in my fashion" is a desperate assertion that dalliance with whores does not really detract from the sincerity and purity of an abiding (but innocent) passion for twelve-year-old girls. Perhaps it does—but anyone who read the poem without having the benefit of Dowson's account of its inspiration would surely find that reading as improbable as it is cynical. If, on the other hand, Dowson's account was a mere mask—a calculated hypocrisy—another interpretation of the poem becomes not merely possible but inviting.

If we look at the poem in this light, it seems obvious that the person, idea or appetite to which the authorial voice of "Cynara" is remaining "faithful in his fashion" is something deep-buried but still festering, anything but an "ideal of innocence". From this viewpoint, the sensible interpretation of the poem's relevance to Adelaide Foltinowicz would be that she—like the owner of the "bought red mouth"—is merely part of the masquerade that licenses and forces the qualification. Perhaps, therefore, her instatement as an inspiration is at least symbolic, if not actually part and parcel, of the false fashion rather than its underlying faithfulness.

If the conventional interpretation of "Cynara" is correct, it is difficult to defend the poet from a charge of flagrant cynicism. If Cynara really were an ideal of innocence, then that ideal really would be besmirched by traffic with whores. But if the ideal to which the poet is being faithful really does require concealment—if the only way he can protect it is by denial—then congress with whores and a declaration of undying love for a legally inaccessible and woefully inappropriate object might both be regarded as faintly heroic as well as ironically perverse. But what secret could Dowson possibly be trying to hide by such an extraordinary device?

No one nowadays, of course, would dream of trying to conceal any kind of perversity by pretending to be a paedophile instead, but the era of Lewis Carroll, John Ruskin, Simeon Solomon and Oscar Wilde was a foreign country in which it made good sense to do things differently. If we look closely at Dowson's life and work, we might take many hints therefrom to support the suspicion that he was using his public declarations of (punctiliously celibate) paedophilia as a mask, and might also hunt for clues as to what it was that he might have felt compelled to conceal.

The one French novel Dowson yearned to translate into English was *Aphrodite* by Pierre Louÿs. The author actually asked for Dowson as his translator, but his request was refused. Dowson presumably knew Louÿs well enough to have seen the entire text as well as the published text, including the chapters that described in lascivious detail all the perversions on sale in the garden where the heroic courtesan plies her trade. Dowson must have understood why Louÿs had felt obliged to write this section, even though he knew full well that it would have to be excluded from the version of the novel offered to the general public (it was circulated *sub rosa* as a dark companion-piece). The subject of the novel is, of course, the irresistibility of a powerful, obsessive, forbidden and altogether arbitrary erotic impulse.

In 1891—the same year that he met Adelaide Foltinowicz and composed "Cynara"—Dowson was converted to Catholicism. (Robert Ross was later to attempt to bring Oscar Wilde into the same fold, although he had to wait until poor Wilde was struck dumb before he finally succeeded in riding roughshod over the dying poet's objections.) Dowson must by then, one assumes, have read Joris-Karl Huysmans' Decadent classic *À rebours*, whose morbidly-obsessed hero commits himself to the church for the appropriately perverse reason that its claims are so obviously delusional. We cannot know whether Dowson agreed with Jean Des Esseintes that the only thing that could be worthy of the faith of a true Decadent was the frankly impossible, any more than we can know whether Huysmans himself agreed with his creation, but we are free to suspect that this too was one more mask, one more defensive bulwark against suspicion.

Readers of "Cynara" who think that the poet's memories are redolent with regrets must suppose that few modifications had taken place by the time he wrote "Absinthia Taetra", in which the absinthe-drinker can find only momentary escape from his nightmares. They must suppose, too, that there is nothing but the straightforward expression of a death-wish in the declaration the narrator of "The Visit" makes to his masked guest: "I have wanted you all my life." But if these interpretations are simplistically true, it is not easy to determine why the absinthe-drinker's past should "[tear] after him like a panther" or why Death should have such "reproachful tenderness...shadowed in his obscure smile" when he replies; "You had only to call."

Both these prose poems were contained in *Decorations* (1899), along with "The Princess of Dreams", which laments the fate of a legendary princess whose liberator never comes. The piece concludes by raising the possibility that she never wanted to be released, and adding the comment that "Some say, moreover, that her tower is not of ivory and that she is not even virtuous nor a princess". Mark Longaker's note in *The Stories of Ernest Dowson* unhesitatingly claims that "This allegory was doubtless written after Adelaide had spurned Dowson's love" but it is possible to put another interpretation on the final words. Perhaps, like Swinburne's Atalanta, the princess is not a princess because "she" is not even female.

If Dowson had not gone to such lengths to establish himself as a romantic paedophile his contemporaries might have suspected that he was possessed of passions of a different stripe, although they would presumably have conceded that they would never be able to determine the exact conformation of those passions. Nor can we—but if we can be convinced that Dowson's mask was a mask, should that not increase rather than decease our admiration for its charm and complexity? And if we can be convinced that Dowson did carry to the grave the secret configuration of his private passions, should we not admire him for his parsimony and fortitude as well as his cleverness?

The English Decadent Movement died on the day Oscar Wilde was committed to prison. W. E. Henley, one of the poets who had fiercely resented the application of the label to himself, declared that everyone in England possessed of "the treasure of a wholesome mind" owed the Marquess of Queensberry a "deep debt of gratitude" and proclaimed that "of the Decadents, of their worse than Eleusinian mysteries, there must be an absolute end." By then, hardly anyone cared to manifest any public support for Wilde, but the one man who did was Ernest Dowson. Apparently, he did not care whether his support for Wilde might awaken the suspicion that he too had dark secrets to hide, any more than he cared whether his professed adoration for a plain child might make him seem ridiculous. And why not, given that his own secret was still his to keep?

Dowson maintained a stubborn presence in court during Wilde's trial, oblivious to his friends' advice that it was unwise to do so. When Wilde left the country following his release from prison Dowson met him in Paris and immediately took him to a brothel—an item of news that the two men took great care to publicize, Wilde being widely quoted as expressing the hopeful belief that the tale would "restore my reputation". Dowson had taken great care to cultivate his own reputation as a regular frequenter of brothels and companion of whores, and he must have known exactly what such a mask was worth to a man's reputation. Dowson wore his own mask so successfully that he could idolize the poetry of Swinburne, maintain a fast friendship throughout his life with Lionel Johnson, and tour Flanders with Conor O'Riordan—subsequently reaping the reward of the dedication of that novelist's *A Fool and His Heart*—without his friends and critics ever suspecting him publicly of dissimulation. Perhaps they were right, and perhaps the truth is stranger than anyone imagines; as things are, though, we must take what perverse delight we can in the awareness that, thanks to Dowson's artifice, we shall never know for sure.

One does, of course, have to respect the opinion of such an adept critic as Thomas Burnett Swann when he seems perfectly certain of the propriety of seconding the conventional account of Dowson's inspiration. It is, however, worth bearing in mind the possibility that even critics sometimes wear masks—and perhaps, therefore, worth wondering whether it is conceivable that Swann's refusal to consider other hypotheses might be a deliberate and sympathetic one. It would require a very clever eye to perceive all the echoes of Swinburne and Dowson that resound in "The Blue Monkeys", the novel—subsequently published in book form as *The Day of the Minotaur*—that was being serialized in *Science-Fantasy* when Swann's study of Dowson was published in the USA, but there is a certain pleasure to be taken in that knowledge that this too must forever remain a matter of fancy and conjecture. Swann—whose other contribution to the Twayne series dealt with that great romanticizer of childhood innocence A. A. Milne—died in 1976; like Ernest Dowson, he never married.

# XVII.

## SHOULD FRANCE'S ANGELS HAVE REVOLTED AFTER ALL?

In the novel translated into English as *The Revolt of the Angels*, Anatole France allegorized the history of post-Revolutionary France in the tale of the Baron d'Esparvieu's library, which was established in Napoleonic times, but fell into neglected in the course of the next hundred years as the Baron's descendants lapsed into political conservatism and religious orthodoxy. The library was consigned by the uncaring René d'Esparvieu to the care of Julien Sariette, who regarded the books as objects to be jealously guarded rather than repositories of wisdom.

France's allegory extended into fanciful realms when Sariette found that books were disappearing and being moved about without any sign of human agency. His anxiety was further amplified when the missing volumes turned up in the apartment of René's son Maurice, although Maurice had no idea how they got there, his own interests being confined to amatory affairs. On further investigation, however, Maurice discovered that the book-thief was his neglectful guardian angel Arcade.

Arcade's studies in natural philosophy and the history of religion had revealed to him that his maker was not the Almighty God he had previously assumed Him to be, but merely a vain and ignorant demiurge named Ialdabaoth, whose sphere of influence was a tiny corner of a much vaster universe. Arcade had also concluded that the microcosm in question was in a rather sorry state, thanks to Ialdabaoth's intolerance and petty tyranny. Arcade confided to Maurice that there were many other lapsed guardian angels living quietly among men, alongside the fallen angels cast out of Heaven long ago by Ialdabaoth; he further opined that it was high time that this fallen legion was gathered together in order to mount a new Revolution against the stubborn power of Heaven.

Embarking upon his crusade, Arcade soon found that most of the angelic defectors were working as teachers and artists. They were, alas, devoid of any conspicuous revolutionary zeal; like Maurice, most of them preferred the pursuit of love to any political activity. Always ready to keep an open mind, Arcade experimented with love himself, borrowing Maurice's current mistress for the purpose, but he found the experience inadequate to his grander ambitions. Persisting in his cause, he eventually found useful allies in the rebel Cherub Prince Istar and the Archangel-formally-known-as-Ithuriel.

Arcade's would-be revolutionaries, enthusiastic to open their campaign with a socialist revolution in France, patiently gathered recruits and arms. Assuming that the armies of the Heavenly Hierarchy must be disorganized and ill-equipped for modern warfare, they were confident of victory. As soon as they were ready they sought out Satan to offer him command of their army and the throne of Heaven—but when Satan was found he declined the offer, no longer having the least desire to rule in Heaven lest he become another Ialdabaoth. Satan was now convinced that his true place was on Earth, carrying forward the causes of liberty, equality and fraternity by stealth.

What would needed in the twentieth century, the greatest and wisest of the fallen angels suggested to Arcade, was not another Revolution to cast the tyrant down from His celestial throne, but rather that the horrid echoes of Ialdabaoth's nature in the minds and hearts of men—His jealousy, His greed, His quarrelsomeness and His violence—should be subdued and ultimately erased by the arts and a love of beauty. In accordance with this advice, Arcade and all other the angels on earth—whether they had fallen or jumped—forsook the cause of Political Revolution in favor of the cause of Moral Evolution.

The question is: were they right to do so?

France's allegory was published in 1914, immediately before the outbreak of the Great War. What role Arcade and his fellow ex-guardians played in that war we do not know; the rumor that they employed English longbows to cover the British retreat at Mons is unsupported by any real evidence. If they were directly involved in the conflict at all, it was probably in the role of ambulance-drivers and stretcher-bearers, but their contribution is more likely to have been indirect. It seems likely that it was a lapsed guardian who invented Salvarsan, the drug that must have saved the Armed Services almost as many lives and minds as the British High Command wasted in cannon-fodder, by providing an effective treatment for syphilis.

What the earthbound angels did when the war was over is less easily deduced. The evidence suggests that few of them went back to the Arts and even fewer to the Academy; the love of beauty has made precious little progress since 1918 and education has grown steadily less effective. In all probability, most of them stayed in Medicine; such moral evolution as we have enjoyed in the last eighty years has been largely the product of better health. We are, however, on safer ground in judging the results of what the renegade angels did not do—the effects of Ialdabaoth's continuing occupation of the throne of Heaven.

Wherever Satan is now (he is probably a genetic engineer) he must be bitterly disappointed by the tenacity with which Ialdabaoth's worst attributes have clung fast to the hearts and mind of men. Avarice, envy, aggression and murder are not in the least diminished—if anything, their infection has spread and their necrotizing effect has increased. An innocent like Arcade (who is presumably no longer innocent, wherever he is now) might be astonished by this, given that the world now has wealth in such abundance that wretchedness could be all-but-abolished. The Arcade of France's allegory would have been astonished to be told that the benefits of increasing wealth would be monopolized by the rich, whose advantage over the poor would be more fiercely guarded the more it increased. How could he be swayed now, if he were to take his proposition to Satan for a second time?

There was, of course, a second element to Satan's argument—which was that anyone who occupied the throne of Heaven would be corrupted by its absolute power, becoming as bad as Ialdabaoth if not worse. That fear has been far better justified than its parallel hope; wherever in the world there have been Revolutions, the new rulers have done little—if any—better than the old. If Moral Evolution has not lived up to our expectations, Satan would probably argue now, Political Revolution has failed more dismally still. Satan, I feel sure, would point to his experiments in genetic engineering and suggest that it is in technological advancement. if it is anywhere, that hope still resides for the sensible assistance of evolution and for the eventual transformation of the world into an Earthly Paradise.

Arcade, I suppose, might be forced to take a different view. "We should not have beaten our swords into timeshares," he would very likely say. "We should not have left Ialdabaoth on the throne of Heaven simply because his replacement would have been no better. We should have toppled him and left the Celestial Throne to rot." In brief, he would probably have abandoned socialism for anarchism. Satan, on the other hand, would probably laugh at Arcade's continued naivety, pointing out that all organizations require administration, and that everything we think of as human is the product of organized collective endeavor. "If you think elected officers are any less inclined to greed and dictatorship than hereditary monarchs," Satan would say to his young pupil, "consider the directors of Camelot, and their bank balances."

What would Arcade elect to do, if he accepted that criticism? In fact, what is he doing? Given that the Cherub Prince Istar and the Archangel-formally-known-as-Ithuriel cannot have perished in Flanders fields, what are they doing now? And what of their enemies, the unlapsed guardian angels?

The unlapsed guardian angels are, of course, an interesting problem in their own right. France and Arcade assumed that all the angels who had not already fallen would eventually jump, as soon as they had learned the truth of their nature and station, but that clearly has not happened. The libraries of the modern world are quieter than the Baron d'Esparvieu's and have fallen into the care of philistines far worse than Julien Sariette. The evidence is overwhelming that the great majority of the guardian angels are as willfully blind as they ever were, and that their stubbornness only increases under the pressure of their rivals' Enlightenment.

We must, with the aid of hindsight, conclude that Ialdabaoth's agents on Earth were alerted to the danger posed by Arcade's crusade as soon as its moment of golden opportunity had passed, and that they must have rearranged their own schemes to take account of the renegades. Strident opposition by the cause of Creationism is one of the main reasons why the course of Moral Evolution has become so messily bogged down—and who could be responsible for that if not the unreformed angels, the terrorists of the imagination?

It may be useful, in attempting to cut through the confusion that afflicts the contemporary predicament of the fallen angels, to remember which book it was that achieved Arcade's conversion. France did not name it explicitly, but left more than enough clues for the reader to deduce that it was *De rerum natura*: Lucretius' classic exposition of the philosophy of Epicurus (all of whose own writings have unfortunately been lost—presumably destroyed by unreformed angels at Ialdabaoth's behest—although his two summary dicta, "Know Thyself" and "Nothing to Excess", are still in circulation). It ought perhaps to be remembered that the main charge laid by *De rerum natura* against any and all gods was not the trivial one of non-existence but the much more serious one of unimportance. According to Epicurus, it did not matter whether the gods existed or not; what mattered was that they were, are and always will be utterly irrelevant to the explanation of the world and the ordering of human conduct.

This insight, I think, gives us an important clue to the strategy that Satan, Arcade and all their allies might now be following in pursuit of their glorious cause. The proper goal of the human heart and the human mind is not to overthrow Ialdabaoth, whether to replace him or to leave his throne forever vacant; the real aim is to secure His utter and absolute insignificance. Such an end can never be achieved by frank and sincere enmity, which only increases the importance of that which is being attacked, whether its form of action is all-out conflict or war of attrition; the objective in question can only be achieved by mockery, whose powers of diminution are unmatched by any other human endeavor.

With this item of information in mind, we may confidently judge that whatever Arcade is doing now, if he is wise, he is doing it sarcastically. Wherever Satan is located now, he must surely be looking at the world with a satirical gaze. No matter what the hosts of Ialdabaoth may do in reply, they have no adequate answer to such a penetrating stare: self-aggrandisement can defend itself against anything except deflation, but deflation leaves it helpless.

We should, of course, be grateful to Arcade and all his kin; their fight is, after all, our fight. Those of us who are unlucky enough still to be stuck with unlapsed guardian angels can best protect our hearts and minds by cultivating a sardonic and corrosive sense of humor. One day, if we can only be patient, they might let us alone—at least, we must certainly hope so.

# Bibliography

[Andreae, J. V.] *Chymische Hochzeit Christiani Rosencreutz*. Strasbourg: 1616 (published anonymously).
Balzac, Honoré (as M. Horace de Saint-Aubin). *Le Centenaire, ou les deux Behirngeld*. Paris: Pollet, 1822. Translated by George Edgar Slusser as *The Centenarian, or the Two Behringelds*. New York: Arno Press, 1976.
———. *Illusions perdues*. Paris: Bureau du Siècle 1854. Translated by Kathleen Raine as *Lost Illusions*. London: John Lehmann, 1951.
———. "Melmoth reconcilié" in *Le Livre des conteurs*. Paris: Lequien, 1835.
———. *Oeuvres complètes*. Paris: Calmann-Lévy, 1900-02.
———. *La Peau de Chagrin*. Paris: Gosselin, 1831.
———. *Le Père Goriot*. Pardis: Werdet, 1835.
———. *Le splendeur et misère des courtisanes*. Paris: L. de Potter, 1845. Translated by James Waring as *A Harlot's Progress*. London: J. M. Dent, 1946.
Baudelaire, Charles. *Les Fleurs du mal*. Paris: Poulet-Malassis, 1857. Translated by Richard Howard as *Les Fleurs du Mal*. London: Harvester Press, 1982.
———. *Oeuvres completes.* 7 vols., Paris: Lévy, 1868-73; extended ed. in 19 vols., Paris: Conard, 1923-65.
———. "Le peintre de la moderne vie." *Le Figaro* novembre 26 & 28, décembre 3. Tranalated by Norman Cameron as "The Painter of Modern Life" in *My Heart Laid Bare and Other Prose Writings*. London: The Soho Book Company, 1986.
———. *Les Paradis artificiels*. Paris: Poulet-Malassis, 1860.
———. *The Poems in Prose, with La Fanfarlo*, translated by Francis Scarfe. London: Anvil Press, 1989.

Beckford, William. *An Arabian Tale*. London: J. Johnson, 1786 (published anonymously). Reprinbted as *Vathek*.

Bertrand, Aloysius. *Gaspard de la nuit: fantaisies à la manière de Rembrandt et de Callot*. Angers: Labitte, 1842. Translated by Donald Sidney-Fryer as *Gaspard de la Nuit*. Encino, CA: Black Coat Press, 2008.

Bodin, Félix. *Le Roman de l'avenir*. Paris: Lecointe et Poucin, 1834. Translated by Brian Stableford as *The Novel of the Future*. Encino, CA: Black Coat Press, 2009.

Burke, Edmund. *A Philosophical Enquiry intioo the Origin of our Ideas of the Sublime and the Beautiful*. London: 1757 (published anonymously).

Burton, Robert. *The Anatomy of Melancholy*. Oxford: John Lichfield and James Short for Henry Cripps, 1621.

Coleridge, Samuel Taylor. "Kubla Khan" in *Christabel; Kubla Khan, a Vision; The Pains of Sleep*. London: Murray, 1816.

Cousin de Grainville, Jean-Baptiste. *Le Dernier homme*. Paris, 1805; tr. as *The Last Man; or, Omegarius and Syderia. A Romance in Futurity*. London: R.Dutton, 1806.

Cros, Charles. *Oeuvres complètes*. Paris: Le Club Français du Livre, 1954. Expended ed. 1964.

Cros, Simon-Charles-Henri. *Théorie de l'homme intellectuel et moral*. 2$^{nd}$ ed. Paris: Bachelier, 1838.

De Quincey, Thomas. *Confessions of an English Opium-Eater*. London: Taylor, 1852.

———. *Confessions of an English Opium-Eater and Suspiria de Profundis*. Boston: Ticknor & Fields, 1856.

———. "On Murder Considered as One of the Fine Arts." *Blackwood's* February 1827.

Dowson, Ernest. "Non sum qualis eram bonae sub regnae Cynarae" in *Verses*. London: Leonard Smithers, 1896.

——— & Arthur Moore. *A Comedy of Masks*. London: Heinemann, 1894.

Doyle, Arthur Conan. *A Study in Scarlet*. London: Ward Lock, 1888.

Du Camp, Maxime. *Souvenirs littéraires*. Paris: Hachette, 1881-82.

Flaubert, Gustave. *Oeuvres completes*. Paris: Conard, 1910-54.

——. *La Première tentation de Saint Antoine*. Paris: Charpentier, 1908. Translated by René Francis as *The First Temptation of Saint Anthony*. London: Duckworth, 1910.

——. *La Tentation de Sainte Antoine*. Paris: Charpentier, 1874. Translated by D. F. Hannigan as *The Temptation of St. Anthony*. London: Nichols, 1895.

Forestier, Louis. *Charles Cros, l'homme et l'oeuvre*. Paris: Minard, 1969

France, Anatole. *L'Abeille*. Paris: Charavay, 1882.

——. *Le Crime de Sylvestre Bonnard*. Paris: Calmann-Lévy, 1881.

——. *L'Étui de nacre*. Paris: Calmann-Lévy, 1892.

——. *L'Île des pingouins*. Paris: Calmann-Lévy, 1908.

——. *Jocaste et the chat maigre*. Paris: Calmann-Lévy, 1879.

——. *Le Lys rouge*. Paris: Calmann-Lévy, 1894.

——. *Le puits de Sainte Claire*. Paris: Calmann-Lévy, 1895. Translated by Alfred Allinson as *The Well of Saint Clare*. London: John Lane, 1909.

——. *La Révolte des anges*. Paris: Calmann-Lévy, 1914. Translated by Winifred Jackson as *The Revolt of the Angels*. London: John Lane, 1914.

——. *Les Sept femmes de Barbe-bleue*. Paris: Calmann-Lévy, 1921.

——. *Sur la pierre blanche*. Paris: Calmann-Lévy, 1905.

——. *Thaïs*. Paris: Calmann-Lévy, 1890.

Gautier, Théophile. Introduction to the third edition of *Les Fleurs du Mal*. In *Charles Baudelaire: His Life* tr. by Guy Thorne. New York: Brentano's, 1915.

——. *Mademoiselle de Maupin*. Paris: E. Renduel, 1835.

——. "Une nuit de Cléopâtre." *La Presse* novembre 29-décembre 6, 1838.

——. *Oeuvres complètes*, 22 vols. Paris: Lévy, 1855-74. Translated by F. C. de Sumichrast as *Complete Works*, 12 vols. Boston: Brainard, 1900.

——. *One of Cleopatra's Nights and Other Stories*, translated by Lafcadio Hearn. New York: Worthington, 1882.

Gawsworth, John, ed. *Crimes, Creeps and Thrills*. London: E. Grant, 1937.

Goncourt, Edmond de. *Chérie*. Paris: Charpentier, 1884.

———. *La Faustin*. Paris: Charpentier, 1882. Translated by G. F. Monkshood and Ernest Tristan as *La Faustin*. London: Greening, 1906.

———. *La Fille Elisa*. Paris: Charpentier, 1877.

———. *Les Frères Zemganno*. Paris: Charpentier, 1879.

Goncourt, Edmond & Jules de. *Germinie Lacerteux*. Paris: Charpentier, 1865.

———. *Henriette Maréchal*. Paris: Librairie Internationale, 1866.

———. *Les Hommes de lettres*. Paris: Dentu, 1860.

———. *Madame Gervaisais*. Paris: Librairie Internationale, 1866.

———. *Manette Salomon*. Paris: Librairie Internatiionale, 1867.

———. *Renée Mauperin*. Paris: Charpentier, 1864.

———. *Soeur Philomène*. Paris: Librairie Nouvelle, 1861.

Gresset, Jean-Baptiste. *Ver-vert, ou les voyages du perroquet de Nevers, poëme héroique*. Paris, 1733.

Hodgson, William Hope. *The Night Land*. London: Eveleigh Nash, 1912.

Hood, Thomas. "The Bridge of Sighs." *Hood's Monthly Magazine and Comic Miscellany* May 1844.

Hugo, Victor. *L'Homme qui rit*. Paris: Libraire Internationale, 1869.

———. *Les Misérables*. Brussels: G. Paetz, 1862.

———. *Notre-Dame de Paris. 1485*. Paris: Gosseilin, 1831.

———. *Oeuvres complètes*. Paris: E. Renduel, 1826.

Huysmans, Joris-Karl. *À rebours*. Paris: Charpentier, 1884. Translated by Robert Baldick as *Against Nature*. Harmondsworth: Penguin, 1959.

———. *À vau l'eau*. Brussels: Kistemaeckers, 1882.

———. *Croquis parisiens*. Paris: Henri Vaton, 1880. Expanded ed. 1886. Translated by Richard Griffiths as *Parisian Sketches*. London: Fortune Press, 1960.

———. *Le Drageoir à épices*. Paris: Dentu, 1874.

———. *En ménage*. Paris: Charpentier, 1881.

———. *Là-Bas*. Paris: Tresse et Stock, 1891. Translated by Keene Wallace as *Down There: Là-Bas*, Paris: prvately printed, 1928.

———. *Marthe, histoire d'une fille*. Brussels: Gay 1876.

———. *Sainte Lydwine de Schiedam*. Paris: Stock, 1901.

———. *Les Soeurs Vatard*. Paris: Charpentier, 1879.

Koestler, Arthur. *The Act of Creation*. London: Hutchinson, 1964.
Lamothe-Langon, Étienne-Léon. *L'Espion de police*. Paris: A. Dupont, 1826.
Longaker, Mark, ed. *The Stories of Ernest Dowson*. London: W. H. Allen, 1947.
Lorrain, Jean. "Dolmancé" in *Sensations et souvenirs*. Paris: Charpentier et Fasquelle, 1895.
——. *Monsieur de Phocas*. Astarté. Paris: Ollendorff, 1901; translated by Francis Amery as *Monsieur de Phocas*. Sawtry: Dedalus, 1994.
Louÿs, Pierre. *Aphrodite: Moeurs antiques*. Paris: Mercure de France, 1896. Translated by Stanley Reynolds as *Aphrodite*. Paris: Borel, 1900.
Maturin, Charles. *Melmoth the Wanderer*. Edinburgh: Constable, 1820.
Maugham, W. Someerset. *Of Human Bondage*. London: Heinemann, 1915.
Mendès, Catulle. *Luscignole*. Paris: Dentu, 1892; translated by Phyllis Mégroz in *Number 56 and Other Stories*. London: Werner Laurie, 1928.
——. *La Maison de la vieille*. Paris: Charpentier, 1894.
Mercer, Mick. *The Hex Files: The Goth Bible*. London: Batsford, 1996.
Montesquieu, Baron de. *Considérations sur the causes de la grandeur des Romains et leur décadence*. Paris, 1774.
Nisard, Desiré. *Histoire de la littérature francaise*. Paris: Firmin-Didot, 1844-61.
——. "M. Victor Hugo en 1836." *Revue de Paris* janvier 1836.
O'Riordan, Conor (as F. Norreys Connell). *A Fool and His Heart*. London: Leonard Smithers, 1896.
Poe, Edgar Allan. *The Narrative of Arthur Gordon Pym of Nantucket*. New York: Harper, 1838 (published anonymously).
——. *Tales of Edgar Allan Poe*. New York: Wiley and Putnam, 1845.
——. *Tales of the Grotesque and Arabesque*. Philadelphia: Lea and Blanchard, 1840.
——. *Works*. 4 vols. New York: John Redfield, 1850-56.

Rimbaud, Arthur. *Oeuvres*. Paris: Mercure de France, 1898.

Rosny, J.-H. aîné. "La Mort de la terre." *Les Anales Politiques et Littéraire* mai-juillet 1910; reprinted in *La Mort de la terre*. Paris: Plon, 1912. Translated by Brian Stableford in *The Navigators of Space and Other Alien Encounters*. Encino, CA: Black Coat Press, 2010.

Rousseau, Jean-Jacques. *L'Émile ou de l'Éducation*. Paris: Firmin Didot, 1762.

Sainte-Beuve, Charles-Augustin. *Volupté*. Paris: Eugène Renduil, 1834. Translated by Marilyn Gaddis Rose as *Volupté: The Sensual Man*. New York: State University of New York Press, 1975.

Shiel, M. P. *Prince Zaleski*. London: John Lane, 1895.

Smith, Clark Ashton. "The Hashish-Eater; or, The Apocalypse of Evil" in *Ebony and Crystal*. Auburn, Cal.: author, 1922.

———. *Tales of Zothique*. Necronomicon Press, 1995.

Stenbock, Eric. *Studies of Death*. London: Nutt, 1894.

Sterling, George. "A Wine of Wizardry." *Cosmopolitan* September 1907.

Swann, Thomas Burnett. *Day of the Minotaur*. New York: Ace, 1966.

———. *Ernest Dowson*. New York: Twayne, 1964.

Taine, Hippolyte. *Histoire de la littérature anglaise*. Paris: Hachette, 1863.

Verlaine, Paul. *Oeuvres complètes*, 6 vols. Paris: Vanier, 1899-1903.

———. *Les Poètes maudits*. Paris: Vanier, 1884; extended ed., 1888.

Vidocq, François. *Mémoires*. Paris: Tenon, 1828-29.

———. *Les Vrais mystères de Paris*. Paris: C. Muquardt, 1844.

Villiers de l'Isle Adam, Comte de. *Contes cruels*. Paris: Calmann-Lévy, 1883. Translated by Hamish Miles as *Sardonic Tales*, New York: Knopf, 1927.

———. *L'Ève future*. Paris: Brunhoff, 1886. Translated by Robert Martin Adams as *Tomorrow's Eve*. Chicago: University of Illinois Press, 1982.

Wilde, Oscar. *The Picture of Dorian Gray*. London: Ward Lock, 1891.

———. "The Sphinx" in *Poems*. Boston: Roberts Bros., 1881.

Zola, Émile. *L'Assommoir*. Paris: Charpentier, 1877.

———. *Le Docteur Pascal.* Paris: Charpentier et Fasquellle, 1893.
———. *La Faute de l'Abbé Mouret.* Paris: Charpentier, 1875.
———. *Thérèse Raquin.* Paris: Lecroix, Verboeckhaven et Cie,1867.

# INDEX

*Abbé Mouret's Transgression* 109
*Abeille, L'* 140
"Absinthia Taetra" 174, 177
"À combien l'amour revient aux vieillards" 55
*Act of Creation, The* 11
*Aesthetika* 55
*Against Nature* 166
*Against the Grain* 166
*Album Zutique, L'* 134
Alexis, Paul 99
Allais, Alphonse 133-134, 138
"Ambulante, L'" 101-102, 104
*Anatomy of Melancholy, The* 34
Andreae, Johann Valentin 19
"Anywhere out of the World" 151, 165
*Aphrodite* 153, 176-177
*À rebours* 7, 63, 97, 101-103, 105, 107, 113, 116-117, 128-129, 134, 140, 166-168, 177
Arman de Caillavet, Madame 143-150
"Arria Marcella, souvenir de Pompeii" 45, 48, 51
*Assommoir, L'* 107, 117
Astruc, Gabriel 134
*As You Like It* 51
*Atalanta in Calydon* 174
Aubernon, Madame 143
Aupick, General 54
Austen Jane 155
*À vau l'eau* 100, 102
"Ballade en prose de la chandelle des six" 101, 103
Balzac, Honoré de 23, 29-30, 54-62, 77

Banks, Joseph 32
Banville, Théodore de 44, 132
Barbey d'Aurevilly, Jules 54, 107
Baudelaire, Charles 8, 11-13, 15-16, 22-27, 29-33, 37-41, 44, 49, 53-54, 59-60, 62-64, 67, 70, 73, 75-77, 82, 85-97, 103, 105, 107-108, 118, 122, 140, 142, 151-154, 164-168, 170
Baumgarten, Alexander 66-67
Beaumarchais, Pierre 132
Beckford, William 38
*Bee* 140
Béranger, Pierre-Jean 23, 88
"Berenice" 86-88, 95
Bernhardt, Sarah 167
Bertrand, Aloysius (or Louis) 64-72, 97
"Bièvre, La" 101-102
Bismarck, Prince 78
*Blackwood's Magazine* 31, 37
Blake, William 26, 74-75
"Blue Monkeys, The" 179
Bodin, Félix 155-160
Bouilhet, Louis 73-75, 83
Bourget, Paul 134
"Bridge of Sighs, The" 151-152, 165
Browne, Sir Thomas 92
Brueghel, Pieter 73-74
Brummell, George "Beau" 54, 165
Brunetière, Fernand 145
*Bug-Jargal* 20
Burke, Edmund 36, 38
Burton, Robert 34
Byron, Lord 54, 153
Callias, Comte Hector de 131, 134
Callot, Jacques 66-67, 71
Campanella, Tommaso 89
Carroll, Lewis 173, 176
"Cask of Amontillado, The" 87
"Cauchemar" 103
Céard, Henri 99
*Centenaire, Le, ou les deux Behringeld* 61
*Centenarian, The; or, The Two Behringelds* 61

"Chambre, double, La" 165-166
"Chant des Hydropathes, Le" 124
*Chants de Crépuscule, Les* 12
*Charles Cros, l'hommme et l'oeuvre* 129
*Chat Noir, Le* 134-135
Chaulnes, Duc de 133
*Chérie* 120
Christian Death 170
*Chymische Hochzeit Christiani Rosenkreutz* 19
*City of the Sun, The* 89
"Clarimonde" 45
"Claudine" 98
Clute, John 154
*Coffret de santal, Le* 132-133
Coleridge, Samuel Taylor 32-33, 86
*Comédie humaine, La* 55, 60-61
Comte, Auguste 14
*Confessions of an English Opium-Eater* 31-41, 125
*Considérations sur les causes de la grandeur des Romains et de leur decadence* 15, 42-43
*Contes cruels* 168
Coppée, François 101, 106, 131, 143
Coquelin, Ernest (Coquelin *cadet*) 133
*Cosmos* 131
Courrière, Berthe 168
Cousin de Grainville, Jean-Baptiste 153
*Crime de Sylvestre Bonnard, Le* 140
*Crime of Sylvestre Bonnard, The* 140
*Crimes, Creeps and Thrills* 104
*Cromwell* 16-17
*Croquis Parisiens* 97-98, 101-106
Cros, Antoine 129-132
Cros, Charles 128-139, 142
Cros, Guy-Charles 133
Cros, Henri 129, 132
Cros, Henriette 129
Cros, Henry 129-130
Cure, The 170
"Cynara" ("Non sum quails eram bonae sub regno Cynarae") 173-177
"Damiens" 104-106

Damiens, Robert 104
Damned, The 170
"Danse des morts, La" 74
"Darkness" 153
Daudet, Alphonse 132
Davy, Humphry 32
*Day of the Minotaur, The* 179
*Décadence, La* 135
*De Carne Christi* 88
*Decorations* 178
"Defence of Poetry, A" 74-75
*Démocratie pacifique, La* 85
De Quincey, Thomas 31-41, 125
Derleth, August 164
*Dernier homme, Le* 153
*De Rerum Natura* 148, 184
*Dernière incarnation de Vautrin, La* 56
Des Esseintes, Jean 7, 63, 67, 71, 97, 103, 107, 112-113, 115-118, 121, 125, 128, 134-135, 140, 149, 166-168, 177
*Deux poètes, Les* 55, 57
*Docteur Pascal, Le* 108, 111, 113-115
"Dolmancé" 121-122
*Downstream* 100
Dowson, Ernest 172-179
*Drageoir à épices, Le* 97-98, 101
"Drame interastral" 132
Drouet, Juliette 12
Du Camp, Maxime 73-75, 83
Dumas, Alexandre 23, 91
Dumas, Alexandre *fils* 143
"Du vin et du haschisch" 33
Edison, Thomas 133
*Éducation sentimentale, L'* 73, 78, 117
*Émile* 156
"End of Evil Ways, The" 55
Endura 170
*En ménage* 102
*Espion de Police, L'* 91
"Esther Happy" 55
"Esther heureuse" 55

*Esther, ou Les amours d'un vieux homme* 55
*Étui de nacre, L'* 146
*Eureka* 87, 93, 95-96
*Ève future, L'* 154
"Evening Service" 67
Ewers, Hanns Heinz 104
"Extase" 98
Eymeric de Gironne 89
"Fall of the House of Usher, The" 87-90, 95
*Faustin, La* 117-118, 120-127
*Faute de l'Abbé Mouret, La* 107-114, 117
*Feuilles d'automne, Les* 12
Feydeau, Ernest 23
Fields of the Nephilim, The 170
*Fille Élisa, La* 120
*First Temptation of Saint Anthony, The* 83
Flammarion, Camille 131
Flaubert, Gustave 23, 62, 66, 73-84, 117, 140, 147-148, 153
*Fleurs du Mal, Les* 11, 13, 22, 31-32, 38-39, 44, 50, 76-77, 86-87, 151, 165
Fludd, Robert 89
Foltinowicz, Adelaide 173-178
*Fool and his Heart, A* 179
"Fop, The" 67
Forestier, Louis 129
France, Anatole (Anatole-François Thibault) 9, 128-130, 140-150, 153, 160, 168, 180-185
Francis, René 83
*Frères Zemmgano, Les* 119
Galas, Diamanda 170
Galland, Antoine 154
Garden of Delight, The 170
*Gaspard de la Nuit* 64-72
Gautier, Théophile 11, 13, 15, 17, 22-23, 32-33, 44-51, 76, 87, 90, 153, 164-165
Gawsworth, John 104
*Gazette Bibliographique, La* 141
*Germinie Lacerteux* 118, 120-121
*Gil Blas* 134
Gill, André 134

*Giselle* 51
*Glorious Perversity: The Decline and Fall of Literary Decadence* 7
*Golden Legend, The* 40
Goncourt, Edmond de 99, 101, 104, 117-127, 1443
Goncourt, Jules de 99, 118-120, 143
"Gothic Chamber, The" 67
Goudeau, Émile 133-134
Gourmont, Remy de 134, 168
"Gousset, Le" 101-104
*Grand homme de province à Paris, Un* 55, 57-58
Gresset, Jean-Baptiste 89
Grisi, Carlotta 51
Grisi, Ernesta 51
*Gros-Caillou* 102
Guérin de Sauville, Valérie 143-144
Gutenberg, Johann 18
Guys, Constantin 53
*Han d'Islande* 20
*Hareng saur, L'* 133
*Harlot's Progress, A* 55
Harris, Frank 173
*Hashish* 32
"Hashish-Eater, The; or, The Apocalpyse of Evil" 40
Hearn, Lafcadio 44-45, 47, 49
Henley. W. E. 178
Hennique, Léon 99
*Henriette Maréchal* 120
*Hernani* 16-17, 90
*Hex Files, The: The Goth Bible* 163
*Histoire de la literature anglaise* 14
*Histoire de la literature française* 13
Hjardemaal, Mary 133
Hodgson, William Hope 153
Holberg, Ludwig 89
Holmes, Augusta 131
*Homme qui rit, L'* 20
*Hommes de lettres, Les* 119
*Honey-Bee* 140
Hood, Thomas 151, 165
"Hour of the Sabbath, The" 68

Hugo, Adèle 24-26
Hugo, Victor 11-12, 16-19, 23-24, 27, 64-65, 90, 108, 147, 153, 155
"Human Tragedy, The" 146
Huysmans, Joris-Karl 7, 37, 63-65, 97-106, 112, 117, 121, 128-129, 134-135, 149, 166-167-168, 171, 177
*Hydropathe, L'* 134
*Île des pingouins, L'* 148
*Illusions perdues, Les* 55, 60
*Illustration, L'* 86
"Imp of the Perverse, The" 87
Incubus Succubus 170
"Invitation au voyage, L'" 165
James, Henry 174
"Jester, The" 68
*Jocasta and The Famished Cat* 140
*Jocasta et le chat maigre* 140
Johnson, Lionel 179
Kant, Immanuel 39
"King Candaules" 45
"Kingdom of the Dwarfs, The" 140
Koestler, Arthur 11, 13
"Kubla Khan" 86
*Là-Bas* 97, 105-106, 168
La Hire, Jean de 154
Lamarck, Chevalier de 29
Lamothe-Langon, Étienne-Léon 90-92
Larousse, Pierre 91-92
Leconte de Lisle, Charles 44, 132, 141, 143
Leibniz, Gottfried 66
Lemaître, Jules 143
Lemerre, Alphonse 141, 143
"Lepers, The" 68
Le Rouge, Gustave 154
Lévi, Éliphas 168
Lévy, Michel 86
*Liberté de Penser, La* 85
*Life of Apollonius of Tyana, The* 45
"Litanies de Satan, Les" 76, 78, 170
*London Magazine, The* 31
Longaker, Mark 178

Lorrain, Jean 68, 118, 121, 125, 167-168
*Lost Illusions* 55
Louis XI 18
Louis XV 104
Louis Napoléon (Napoléon III) 78, 99
Louis-Philippe 91
Louÿs, Pierre 153, 176-177
Lovecraft, H. P. 36, 95, 164, 170
Loynes, Comtesse de 143
"Lucifer" 146
Lucretius 148, 184
"Luscignole" 153-154
*Lys rouge, Le* 146
Machiavelli, Niccolo 89
"Machine à changer la charactère des femmes, La" 133
*Madame Bovary* 75-77, 81-82, 119
*Madame Gervaisais* 120
*Mademoiselle de Maupin* 50-51, 87
*Maison de la vieille, La* 130
Mallarmé, Stéphane 30, 63-64, 70, 71, 97, 103, 132, 141-142, 167, 169
Manet, Édouard 103
*Manette Salomon* 119-120, 143
Marie Antoinette 92
*Marthe, histoire d'une fille* 99
"Masque of the Red Death, The" 87, 89-90
Maturin, Charles 61
Maugham, W. Somerset 173
Maupassant, Guy de 99
Mauté, Madame 132
*Mécanique cérébrale* 132
"Melmoth reconcilié" 61
"Melmoth Reconciled" 61
*Melmoth the Wanderer* 61
Mendès, Catulle 99, 130-131, 141-142, 153-154
Mercer, Mick 163-164, 169-170
Mercier, Henri 132
"Mesmeric Revelation" 85, 87-88, 94-95
*Messager de l'Assemblée. Le* 31
 "Metzengerstein" 87-88, 95
Meunier, Isabelle 85

*Mille-et-une nuits, Les* 154
Milne, A. A. 179
Milton, John 26, 74
*Misérables, Les* 17
"Moine bleu, Le" 133
*Moniteur universel, Le* 86
Monkshood, G. F. 122, 124
*Monsieur de Phocas* 168
Montesquieu, Baron de 15, 42-45, 50
Montesquiou, Robert de 60, 103, 167
Moore, Arthur 174
Moreau, Gustave 103
Moreau, Joseph 32
"Mort de la Terre, La" 153
"Morte amoureuse, La" 45, 48
*Mother of Pearl* 146
"Mummy's Foot, The" 45
"Murder Considered as One of the Fine Arts" 41
"Murders in the Rue Morgue, The" 87, 90-95, 163-164
Musset, Alfred de 31
*Mystères de Paris, Les* 91
"Mystery of Marie Roget, The" 95
*Naked Truth* 9
*Narrative of A. Gordon Pym, The* 86, 166
"Night and her Glamours" 67
*Night Land, The* 153
*Night Thoughts* 34
Nisard, Desiré 11-13, 15-18, 21
Nodier, Charles 11, 17, 23-24, 65, 155
*Notre Dame de Paris—1482* 16-21, 153
*Nouvelle Héloïse, La* 94
*Nouvelles fleurs du mal* 141
*Nouvelles histories extraordinaires* 86
"Nuit de Cléopâtre, Une" 44-52, 153
"Obsession, L'" 104
*Of Human Bondage* 173
*Old Goriot* 55
"Omphale" 45, 48
"Ondine" 68
*One of Cleopatra's Nights and Other Fantastic Romances* 44-45

*On the Origins of our Ideas of the Sublime and the Beautiful* 38
"On the Rocks of Chèvre-Mort" 69
O'Riordan, Conor 179
*Ou mènent les mauvais chemins* 55, 58
"Painter of Modern Life, The" 53
*Paphnuce* 144
*Paradis artificiels, Les* 31, 33-34, 38
*Parisian Sketches* 97
*Parnasse contemporain, Le* 129-131, 133, 141-142
*Pavillon des fantômes, Le* 134
*Pays, Le* 87
*Peintre de la moderne vie, Le* 53-54
*Peau de chagrin, La* 29, 61
Péladan, Joséphin 168
Pellatan, Camille 134
*Penguin Island* 148
*Penny Dreadfull, The* 9
Père France 141
*Père Goriot, Le* 55-57, 61
Perrault, Charles 154
*Phaedre* 122
*Philosophie dans la boudoir, La* 121
"Philosophy of Composition, The" 86
Philostratus 45
*Picture of Dorian Gray, The* 168
"Pied de momie, Le" 45, 48
"Pit and the Pendulum, The" 86
Poe, Edgar Allan 9, 25, 85-96, 163-166, 169
*Poètes maudits* 134, 142, 166
Pomponius Mela 89
*Presse, La* 32
"Princess of Dreams, The" 178
*Prince Zaleski* 169
"Procurateur de Judea, Le" 146
"Procurator of Judea, The" 146
"Provincial Celebrity in Paris, A" 55
*Le Puits de Sainte Claire* 146
Queensberry, Marquess of 178
Racine 122
Radcliffe, Ann 29

*Rapin, Le* 134
*Red Lily, The* 146
Redon, Odile 103
Rembrandt van Rijn 66-67, 71
*Renaissance littéraire et artistique, La* 132
*Renée Mauperin* 119-120
*République des Lettres, La* 99
"Rêve d'enfer" 74
*Revolt of the Angels, The* 148, 168, 180-185
*Révolte des Anges, La* 148-150, 168, 180-185
*Revue de Paris* 85-86
*Revue des Deux Mondes, La* 145
*Revue du Monde Nouveau* 128, 132
*Revue Française* 38
Ricard, Louis-Xavier de 141
Richepin, Jules 131, 134
Rimbaud, Arthur 70, 132, 166
"Ritournelle" 98
"Rive gauche, La" 98-99, 102
Robida, Albert 134
*Robinson Crusoe* 156
Rohan, Cardinal de 92
"Roi Candaule, Le" 45, 48
*Roman de l'avenir, Le* 155, 157
Rops, Félicien 103
Rosny *aîné*, J.-H. 142, 147, 153-154
Ross, Robert 177
Rousseau, Jean-Jacques 27, 94, 155-156
Ruskin, John 173, 176
Sade, Marquis de 121
Sainte-Beuve, Charles-Augustin 12, 23-30, 64-65, 67, 122
*Sainte Lydwine de Schiedam* 100
"Saint-Satyr" 146
"Salamander, The" 68
*Salammbô* 77-78
Salis, Rodolphe 134
*Scapin, Le* 135
"Scarbo" 68
Schwob, Marcel 168
"Science de l'amour, La" 128, 132, 134-138

*Science-Fantasy* 179
"Second Man, The" 69
*Sept femmes de Barbe-Bleue et autres contes merveilleux, Les* 148
"Serenade, The" 67
*Seven Wives of Bluebeard and Other Marvellous Tales, The* 148
Shakespeare, William 51
Shelley, Percy Bysshe 74
Shiel, M. P. 169
Sidney-Fryer, Donald 64, 69
"Similitudes, Les" 102-103
*Sin of Abbé Mouret, The* 109
"Smarh" 74
Smith, Clark Ashton 40, 103, 153, 172
*Soeur Philomène* 119-120
*Soeurs Vatard, Les* 100, 102
Solomon, Simeon 176
"Song of the Mask, The" 68
*Souffrances de l'inventeur, Les* 55, 58
*Souvenirs littéraires* 73
"Souvenirs of an Egotist" 173
"Sphinx, The" 40
*Spirite, nouvelle fantastique* 51-52
*Spleen de Paris* 86, 165
*Splendeurs et misères de courtesans* 55, 58-59, 61
*Splendors and Miseries of Courtesans, The* 55
Stenbock, Count Stanislaus Eric 169
Stendhal 23
Sterling, George 40, 64
*Stories of Ernest Dowson, The* 178
*Studies in Death* 169
*Study in Scarlet, A* 169
Sue, Eugène 91-92
"Sufferings of an Inventor, The" 55
Sumichrast, F. C. 47
*Sur la pierre blanche* 148
*Suspiria de Profundis* 31, 36-39, 41
Swann, Thomas Burnett 172, 179
Swedenborg, Emmanuel 89
Swinburne, Algernon 168, 174, 178
Taine, Hippolyte 14-16

*Tales from a Mother-of-Pearl Casket* 146
*Temps, Le* 143
*Tentation de Saint Antoine, La* 66, 73-84, 117, 148, 153
Tertullian 88
*Thaïs* 144-145, 147-149, 153
*Théorie de l'homme intellectual et moral* 129
*Thérèse Raquin* 119
Tieck, Ludwig 89
"To a Bibliophile" 68
*Torpille, La* 55, 57
*Tout-Paris* 134
"Tragédie humaine, La" 146, 148
Tristan, Ernest 122, 124
"Two Poets" 55
*Univers Illustré, L'* 143
Varlet, Théo 154
*Vathek* 38
"Vautrin's Last Avatar" 56
Verlaine, Matilde 132
Verlaine, Paul 64, 118, 131-132, 134-135, 141-142, 166
Verne, Jules 134
*Ver-vert* 89
Vidocq, François-Eugène 90-92
Vigny, Alfred de 23, 141
Villard, Nina de (Nina de Callias) 130-134, 142-143
Villiers de l'Isle Adam, Comte de 63, 95-96, 118, 128-129, 131, 132-133, 135, 138, 154, 168
*Volupté* 12, 23-30, 122
"Voyage, Le" 38-40, 151, 153
*Vrais mystères de Paris* 91
Wagner, Richard 12
*Well of Saint Clare, The* 146
Wells, H. G. 154
"What Love Costs an Old Man" 55
*White Stone, The* 148
Wilde, Oscar 8, 40, 50, 87, 168-169, 172, 176-179
"Wine of Wizardry, A" 40
*Works of Théophile Gautier, The* 47
*Wormwood* 7-9
"Yet Another Springtime" 69

Young, Edward 34
Zola, Émile 99-102, 105, 107-117, 119, 132, 143

# ABOUT THE AUTHOR

**BRIAN STABLEFORD** was born in Yorkshire in 1948. He taught at the University of Reading for several years, but is now a full-time writer. He has written many science fiction and fantasy novels, including *The Empire of Fear*, *The Werewolves of London*, *Year Zero*, *The Curse of the Coral Bride*, *The Stones of Camelot* and *Prelude to Eternity*. Collections of his short stories include a long series of *Tales of the Biotech Revolution*, and such idiosyncratic items as *Sheena and Other Gothic Tales* and The *Innnsmouth Heritage and Other Sequels*. He has written numerous nonfiction books, including *Scientific Romance in Britain, 1890-1950*, *Glorious Perversity: The Decline and Fall of Literary Decadence*, *Science Fact and Science Fiction: An Encyclopedia* and *The Devil's Party: A Brief History of Satanic Abuse*. He has contributed hundreds of biographical and critical entries to reference books, including both editions of *The Encyclopedia of Science Fiction* and several editions of the library guide, *Anatomy of Wonder*. He has also translated numerous novels from the French language, including several by the feuilletonist Paul Féval and numerous classics of French scientific romance by such writers as Albert Robida, Maurice Renard, and J. H. Rosny the Elder.

www.ingramcontent.com/pod-product-compliance
Lightning Source LLC
LaVergne TN
LVHW041617070426
835507LV00008B/292